AROUND AUST

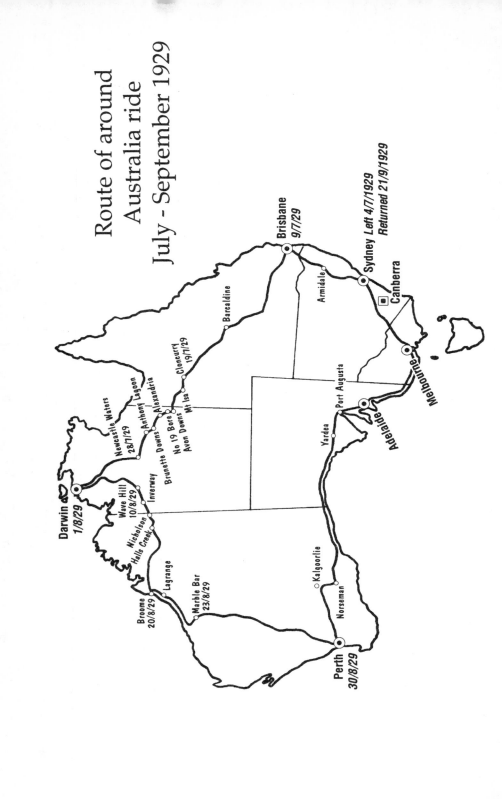

Route of around
Australia ride
July - September 1929

Brisbane
9/7/29

Sydney *Left 4/7/1929*
Returned 21/9/1929

Canberra

Armidale

Barcaldine

Cloncurry
19/7/29

Mt Isa

Port Augusta

Anthony Lagoon
Alexandria

Newcastle Waters
28/7/29

No 19 Bore
Avon Downs
Brunette Downs

Yardea

Adelaide

Melbourne

Darwin
1/8/29

Inverway

Wave Hill
10/8/29

Nicholson
Halls Creek

Lagrange

Kalgoorlie

Broome
20/8/29

Marble Bar
23/8/29

Norseman

Perth
30/8/29

Around Australia the Hard Way

JACK BOWERS

Kangaroo Press

To the memory of
Frank Oakley Smith

Reprinted in 1996
First published in 1995 by Kangaroo Press Pty Ltd
3 Whitehall Road Kenthurst NSW 2156 Australia
PO Box 6125 Dural Delivery Centre NSW 2158
Printed by Australian Print Group, Maryborough, Victoria 3465

ISBN 0 86417 682 1

Contents

Foreword

THE CURRENT RECORD for riding a motorcycle around Australia is less than a week. Think about that for a moment; the distance is about 15,000 kilometres. The Auto Cycle Union of Australia, who supervised the journey chronicled in this book, and *Motorcycling Australia* have long since stopped supervising and thereby supporting such rides. I know some of the people who have steadily brought the record down to its current, absurdly low time and without exception they are driven people, consumed by the need to prove themselves.

Then consider Jack Bowers and Frank Smith. They decided to go out and set the first around-Australia motorcycle record because it was 'interesting'; when it became apparent that they wouldn't be able to raise any financial support they thought they'd go anyway and 'make it a holiday'.

No doubt many people thought they were mad when they set out, but to me Jack and Frank seem like the sanest and most amiable of men. They saw a challenge in a time that was dark, and getting darker. And instead of souring with the times and giving in to the gloom that was spreading everywhere with the Great Depression, they bought themselves a motorcycle and a sidecar and set off to do something nobody had ever done before and also, I suspect, to have some fun.

They had fun, too, through the many amazing adventures in this book. And they remained friends, an achievement that rivals the success of their eleven week trip through conditions that must have tried their tempers to the breaking point.

How do I know? Well, in the spirit of Jack and Frank my friend Charlie and I did something similar a couple of decades ago. We didn't face nearly the difficulties that these two handled so wonderfully well, but we did ride a couple of small Honda XL250 trail bikes around the world. Charlie and I are still friends too, but it was a damn close thing at times! The example of mateship set by Jack and Frank is one of the most inspiring memories you will take away from this book.

But there are many other things in the book that you'll have a job forgetting. Like the regular meals our pair depended upon to keep them going on their journey. Fried flour and water dough for breakfast, spread with treacle; and boiled flour and water dough for lunch, also spread with treacle. I blush with shame when I recall complaining about the food on my trip. It was gourmet tucker compared to flour and water dough!

Probably the most impressive thing about this whole project is that Jack and Frank simply had no idea what awaited them. They were aware of the hardship of the trip, more or less, but they often didn't know where their next drink of water or gallon of petrol would come from. That might not seem like much of a problem when you're sitting at home reading a book, but when you're in a similar position you soon find the uncertainty becomes very dispiriting. It did for me, anyway, in places like the Dasht-i-Dargo and the Sahara. But it didn't seem to be a problem for Jack and Frank, even in places that were a lot wilder at the time than either of those relatively tame deserts. Like the main track from Katherine to Darwin, which they actually mapped for the first time!

There are other, similar stories to this one, of amazing journeys and steadfast resolve. But few have such unassuming and likeable heroes. Jack, Frank and their Harley-Davidson have equal places in this book, and they deserve them. And of course there is the fact that this is a book about not just any journey, but a motorcycle journey. And I just happen to think that travelling by motorcycle is by far the best way to get about. Jack and Frank would agree, I think, but if their bike could talk I wouldn't blame it if it said otherwise . . .

PETER 'The Bear' THOEMING
Writer and motorcyclist

1

Early Days

MY FATHER CAME from Ireland—from the outskirts of Waterford where the Bowers family had lived since the year thirteen
hundred and something. Here they had been given a large tract
of land at a place called Fiddown, a small country town with
one hotel about ten miles out of Waterford. And there they are
to this day.

My forebears crossed from England to Ireland when the
English first sought to quell the Irish. Over the centuries it was
forbidden for any Englishman to intermarry with the Catholic
Irish, and this is why and where all the trouble started.

Last century, my grandfather defied this convention and
married my grandmother—Bridget O'Mara. Now nothing
could be more Irish—or Catholic—than a name like that so
my great-grandfather, proud of his heritage, said, 'You
ungrateful dog—leave my roof', or words to that effect, and
my grandmother, being Irish, and most probably obstinate,
saw to it that her Anglo-Irish husband kept well away from
Gregor-Vine, the old family home.

Gregor-Vine is still there, standing on its own estate of
several hundred acres, and one of my distant relatives—
Edward Bowers—lives there still. One of his sisters lives not
more than a mile away in Fiddown House—a large home of
three stories and about forty rooms set in spacious grounds not
far from the family church, which is now in a derelict condition. There are several other homes at Fiddown, all on the
original estate.

Banned from Gregor-Vine, my grandfather never returned
to the family home, nor did any of his progeny. My father,
forbidden to fraternise with his cousins, came to Australia and

1

New Zealand when he was nineteen, and liked what he saw. He returned to Ireland and, being by then somewhat of an adventurer, was invited to the ancestral home to tell his relatives of his adventures in such an outlandish place as Down Under.

True to his parents' teaching, he never crossed the entrance gateway but told of his exploits in this far-off land on the threshold of the family estate. I suppose that is what is known as the Irish independence.

Over one hundred years later, my eldest daughter was the first member of the Australian Bowers family to enter the forbidden land. She was followed some years later by my second daughter, and finally by myself.

None of the Irish Bowers knew there was an offshoot of the family tree in Australia, but there was no need for me to prove I was not an imposter when I visited Fiddown. I was an exact replica of my long-lost relations, and as they took me around the various homes of the district, where each in his turn has been allotted a portion of the original family estate, they exhibited me as if I had arisen from the dead. Their wives said, 'He's just the same as the rest of them'. 'He has the same Bowers family characteristics.'

I had that same look and stature, the same coloured eyes, and the same independence—for I had booked my accommodation in Waterford before I went to visit them.

As I said, my father liked what he saw of Australia. He returned there, and this time he stayed, mainly I suppose because he married my mother—a second-generation Australian.

By 1905 they had five children, each one born in a different location. Apparently despite his marriage my father still had that wanderlust. However, when I was only five my father had two paralytic strokes, which needless to say put a permanent stop to his meanderings from one state to another. In addition to being partially paralysed down the left side, he also suffered from loss of memory of current-day affairs. His memory retained events that had occurred prior to his illness, but he

2

would never talk freely of his earlier years and all the information I have of this part of his life came from my mother and an Irish woman who lived near us when we moved to Sydney.

Due to my father's sudden illness my mother was obliged to struggle for an existence with five children, the eldest of whom was nineteen and the youngest—me—five. I had two sisters and two brothers.

According to family tradition, the eldest male child was named Thomas, the second Edward and the next John. However, my mother did not favour John and quietly had me christened Jack instead. She had her own Australian way of doing things in this regard. My eldest brother was christened Thomas Michael O'Mara—Thomas being the traditional name, Michael my father's name and O'Mara my grandmother's maiden name. But then, unbeknown to others, my mother also included a fourth given name—Horace. What a shock my brother received when, aged about fifty, he first saw his birth certificate.

I still wonder why my second given name is Adolphus. I have long since swept this under the carpet and merely tolerate my other given name, Leo, which does not come from the Latin *leo* (a lion) but from the Pope, Leo XIII. Whenever I have to fill in a declaration I cannot get past Adolphus.

But all that is beside the point, for at the age of five I didn't have a cracker and had no prospects whatever. I don't think I had a pair of shoes until I was ten or twelve.

Despite all those names our mother had bestowed upon us, I was simply called 'Son' by my two brothers. And Son had to bow to the wishes and commands of not only these two much older brothers but also to those of my two sisters. My mother was too busy trying to eke out an existence by going out to do washing and ironing, or sitting in on some confinement or other, to administer much authority in the home. So I became a kind of loner, and thus I grew up.

Deep down I was endowed with my father's genes—including the one that governs wanderlust—and those of his forebears, tempered with the early effects of restraints placed upon

3

my upbringing by a state of poverty. I was always aware of the fact that I had no shoes, and once when I was called upon to step forward in front of the assembled schoolchildren to unfurl the Australian flag on some national day or other, I knew full well that the seat of my pants was so worn the lining shone through like some sort of distress signal—which it really was, I suppose.

I realise now that my sensitivity had nothing to do with me. It was something I had inherited and I just had to bear with it long enough, for I would master this shortcoming one day.

In time, I learned that minor things mattered little. I learned that the influence of other people—quite often total strangers—had a far greater bearing on my life. Now I simply get an idea, allow it to take root, nourish it from time to time, and do nothing—absolutely nothing. Things simply evolve from that individual thought and drop into place. No effort on my part is obvious, even to me. When things go well it is almost as if someone up there likes me.

As an illustration of this, one day I was sitting quietly alone outside a telephone booth in Honolulu. I had just phoned for a cab when along came a woman who, obviously unwittingly, claimed my cab. I told her she would have to pick up the phone and call—as I had done. She apologised, 'And by the way,' I added, 'you are an Aussie.' Then followed the usual chat as one Aussie to another, during which I learned she was a hairdresser on a passenger-freighter. Where it went to I did not determine, nor was I intensely interested. But I did get the name of that ship, and beyond that little more.

Some weeks later I thought I'd find out more about that ship and rang the agents in Honolulu. 'Oh,' said the girl, 'she just came in this morning. She sails at 4 p.m. today.' 'Can I go aboard?' I said. 'Yes, you won't need a pass, just go and look around.' At 1 p.m. I ventured aboard, liked what I saw, and at 4 p.m. as she left Honolulu I was a passenger on a five-week cruise. I was the only Australian amongst seventy Americans, most of whom had booked months in advance. They were

4

astonished to know that I had just walked aboard that very day, paid my fare, and there I was.

How simply is one's life changed from one day to the next by other people's intervention. I joined that ship five times over the next four years. It became my winter home for six weeks every year, and I made numerous friends throughout the U.S.A. amongst the people I met each voyage.

At any rate, in 1910 my mother's sister—Aunt Cis—lived at Miranda, in Sydney, in a four-roomed shack built of round bush timber supports and walled with flattened-out kerosene tins. The partition walls were of hempen bags coated with whitewash. The main living room was crudely furnished with an assortment of cane-bottomed chairs with broken cane trailing downwards towards the earth floor. The family table was proudly introduced as being of pure cedar, but the two boards comprising the top had opened up due to age and over the years had filled up with a mixture of grease and dirt.

Aunt Cis was a strange person. Considerably older than my mother, she had reddish coloured hair which was nearly always hanging down in complete disarray. It seemed she could not care less.

At mealtimes she always occupied a cane-bottomed rocking chair and would sit at table, book in one hand and favourite fork in the other, rocking back and forth and reading during the entire course of the meal. Now and again she would be obliged to attend to whatever was on the fire and would take a step or two to the open fireplace, the surround of which was also regularly painted with whitewash. What fascinated me as a child were the numerous heavy chains hanging down from some mysterious anchorage up the stone chimney. Each chain ended with a hook just above the burning logs, and upon these were suspended various cast-iron cooking vessels, including a large kettle.

Aunt was also an authority on most subjects and in time taught my two sisters all the feminine arts and crafts, such as knitting socks, crocheting and tatting. She was also very keen on bee-keeping and at times had attended an agricultural college solely to learn more about the craft. Usually there was a net bag full of honeycomb hanging above the old cedar table, on which was a receptacle into which the honey would drip, drip, drip all day. To the outside of the net bag would cling all types of flies, bees and other sweet-toothed insects.

Uncle Bill, her husband, was a Welshman who smoked a curved-stem pipe with a swivel cover. He never entered into the general family conversation much at all, but now and again he would sit in his favourite chair—a broken-down old lounge chair—look absently out of the window across the bay and tell some story in a hesitant manner. At times he would pause in mid-sentence, again look out the window, yawn a time or two, and I would wonder why the story had ended. But no—after that pause, and maybe swivelling the lid on his pipe around to enable him to poke at the tobacco with his index finger, he would resume where he had left off. I remember once as a small boy I became so engrossed in Uncle's story that during one of those long silences I stammered, 'Unc, uncle—c'can't get it out.' Maybe the rest of the family wondered the same thing, but nobody said a word.

Or maybe nobody except me was interested because my five cousins, ranging down through the ages of twenty to my age, would invariably have emulated their mother by also bringing their books to the meal table, along with his or her favourite fork—they all had a favourite knives and forks of varying shapes and sizes. Now and again one or the other would glance around, and possibly recognising one of the novels in hand, would say without any preamble whatsoever, 'What do you think of Algernon?' I would hastily look around for Algernon, but after a while I learned that Algernon, or whoever, was one of the characters of the novel.

Cousin Bill, the eldest boy, became so carried away with his books that he once announced that, little was it known, but he was a member of the Secret Service. The strangest part of it all was that the rest of the family seemed to believe him.

They were indeed a strange family, yet every school holiday I enjoyed spending carefree days with my cousins, when Aunt would take us all to the beach and help us gather seashells and then teach us how to make them up into necklaces by stringing them onto a strand of twine. She was a remarkable person.

At the time of my father's sudden illness my family was living in Perth, where I was born. Aunt Ciss wrote and said, 'Pack up and come east. You can settle down on my land.'

Mum and we five children moved into two tents and lived on Aunt's seven acres at Miranda for the next twelve months. We later moved to a five-acre block of virgin land at East Hills, upon which Mum had placed a small deposit. Here we lived in the same two tents until my brothers could build a more permanent structure of two rooms.

The walls of that building were built of split logs, hewn from the standing trees on the property. These logs were split from the fallen tree which had to be firstly sawn into the required length and then split with mall and steel wedges. Each section was about eight inches wide in a rough plate, but by the time the rough and splintery timber had been trimmed with the adze it presented a more finished appearance and fitted quite snugly to its neighbour. The lining on the inside walls was covered with hessian tacked to the slabs of timber and eventually covered with cheap wallpaper. This kept the breeze from infiltrating through cracks between the upright sections of timber.

The floor was of packed earth approximately six inches higher than the ground outside and was covered with a tarred felt material called malthoid to combat the rising dampness. This was later covered with a cheap patterned oilcloth floor material.

One room was what nowadays might be termed as the family room, and here was the wood-burning stove tucked away in one corner and the family piano, which had been brought with us from Western Australia, in the opposite one. In the centre of this room were a table and cane-bottomed chairs, and a wired-in safe holding the essential food. There was also an old-fashioned dresser for the crockery, and a sewing machine.

The second room was the bedroom, occupied by my mother

and my two sisters, then aged eleven and eight. A curtain substituted for a door between the rooms. Doors were not for us except for the front and rear entrances.

I spent most of my boyhood days in a world of fantasy. Most of the years between the age of eight and twelve I was a Red Indian, and stepped quietly and furtively along the bush tracks of my boyhood, ever on the alert for hostile Indians. I was an avid reader of *Deerfoot on the Prairie, Deerfoot on the River* and *Deerfoot on the Mountain.* I knew, and practised, every move that Deerfoot made. I would stalk the family cow with bow and arrow, or from time to time lassoo the cow, then panic and spend the next hour frantically trying to catch the animal to remove the signs of my folly before I was discovered.

I read *The Coral Island* so often that even at that tender age I became, more or less, an authority on coral islands. One of those islands of the Pacific I drooled over as a boy was an atoll. What a magic word that sounded to me! Years later, the atoll of Majuro dispelled all those boyhood fancies and cured me of my love for lonely islands.

Mine might have been a humble and poverty-stricken beginning but I had known no other. Being the youngest, I was obliged to do all the menial chores around the home. 'Jack, we're out of kerosene, you'll have to run over to Jimmy Spence's and get some more.' 'Go and find the cow and calf and put the calf in the pen tonight, and while you're at it, don't forget to get the morning sticks for the fire.' 'The woodbox is low. Go and get another armful.'

So off I would trot—always at the trot; I could, and did, trot for miles—over to the little store one and a half miles away for the bottle of kerosene. I would trot to this store in the gathering dusk, taking every short cut through the bush hoping to get back home before dark. We needed the kerosene for the oil lamp; otherwise we would have to see the night through by candlelight.

Always barefoot. I had no shoes. I went to school barefoot. Despite this, I never missed a single day in four years, for which I received a gold medal from the headmaster each year. The school was about one and a half miles from home and for the best part I had to walk along a rutted cart track winding and twisting amongst the trees.

Jimmy Spence sold just about everything at his store. He sold the newspapers, served as the local post officer and bank officer, and carried a huge variety of household and farming commodities, all of which he handled himself and stacked higgledy-piggledy in that tiny shop.

Jimmy, a middle-aged short-sighted individual, would appear from behind a high stack of boxes and peer around the corner to see who was there. "Yes boy,' he would almost whisper, 'what can I get for you?' Then he might disappear for a moment or two behind his boxes, reappear and slowly, with deliberate and infinite care, look for the article requested. What lay beyond that stack of boxes I never did determine. That precinct would be the living quarters no doubt, but I have never met anyone who had ever seen inside.

Occasionally Jimmy's wife, whose life seemed to exist solely beyond that pile of stacked boxes, would peep around the corner to see who was in the shop and timidly say, 'Hullo boy, and how is your mother?' Having received the answer, she would quietly disappear again.

I don't think anybody ever saw either of the Spences beyond the confines of that jumble of butterboxes, bags of flour and sugar, and the many other items of household requirements.

The only other store in this district was at least another mile further on, and if Jimmy happened to be out of some commodity I would have to clamber over a stile through private property, pass through the local School of Arts grounds and jog on to the Nevilles' store. Here Mrs Neville and her two daughters held sway. Each was moderately tall and thin. Each had her hair swept up from all points to meet at the top of the cranium where a flat bun was formed to keep the hair in place and to flout the laws of gravity. Around each slim neck was a high lace collar extending to a point just below the jawbones. A slim vertical support on each side held this collar in an upright and tidy fashion. Everything was done in meticulous order. Their voices were just as meticuluous and they spoke most politely, but almost in whispers.

'Yes, and what can I get for you?' they would whisper. 'Thankyou.' (This with added emphasis.) 'Now would that be all?' Again the 'thankyou' and here the items would be jotted down on a piece of paper, the pencil appearing from that bun of hair in some mysterious fashion. The amount would be carefully totted up. Twice. 'Now that will be three and fourpence halfpenny. Thankyou. One halfpenny change. Thankyou. Goodbye.'

With my purchases dropped into a sugarbag I would trot back home. Here my second sister and I did our homework while my older brothers, with my oldest sister as accompanist, went over the music of their choice. This was almost an evening's regular routine.

Occasionally the lamp chimney would break due to the sudden heat caused turning the wick up too soon, and off I would trot to the store for a new chimney. Sometimes the outdoor hurricane lamp was used as a temporary stand-by.

My brothers and I slept in a detached building that had been built twenty feet from the main one and on rainy nights one simply had to run the gauntlet through the intervening space. This was my home for fourteen years.

Here at East Hills my brothers established a poultry farm as a sideline to their ordinary clerical work. My eldest brother was also a part-time violin teacher and a member of the Sydney Royal Philharmonic Society. It was always strange to me to see him going off to a full dress rehearsal in his white tie and tails, his violin strapped to his back as he pedalled off on a pushbike to the train at Bankstown, the tails of his coat flapping frenziedly in the breeze.

My father had a good musical background, which was passed on to his children. My other older brother was quite an accomplished flautist and my eldest sister an excellent classical pianist. At the age of six I was provided with a half-size violin and forced to practise one hour each day.

At the age of sixteen I left high school. I was not meant to be an academic. My mind and thoughts were far too active on other subjects. On the pretext of studying history, I would prop an adventure novel against the open pages of my history text and become completely engrossed until a hand would suddenly descend over my shoulder and calmly take my adventure book away. I was a bright boy, but the history teacher was far brighter.

It was decided I should learn a trade and I was fortunate enough to become apprenticed to a large building firm in the city. To get to the city by half past seven each morning, I had to ride a pushbike the four miles to the nearest railway station at Bankstown to catch the six-twenty train. So I would rise at five, light the fuel stove, cook my own breakfast and be on the road before six—hail, rain or shine. I would rouse my sisters as I left as a parting shot, for they, being office workers, did not commence work until nine. Even they had to walk a full mile to catch the bus to the railway station.

My employers paid me eleven shillings a week for the first year, and it increased at the rate of about three shillings per year for the six years I was an apprentice. I received no annual holidays during that period, and any sickness or days off had to be made up at the end of my time.

I commenced my trade course lectures at the Sydney Technical College on the same evening that I started work. Classes began at 7 p.m., so I had to fill in two hours each evening after work. Lectures ended at nine. I would then catch the nine-twenty train from Central Station and arrive back at Bankstown at 10 p.m., walk through a narrow bush track to where I had housed my bike each day at a cost of sixpence per week, then ride the four miles home. I did this three to four nights each week for the next four years.

However, there were always four or five other apprentices living in my area and it was not a lonely ride for most of the journey. On rainy nights it almost became fun to become drenched as we rode our bikes along that dark, muddy, uneven road.

Quite often during the cold winter months I would arrive

home at ten-thirty, wet to the skin, arise again the next morning and repeat the performance. However, in time I grew sick and tired of riding that pushbike to and from the railway station and made a down payment on my first motorbike, a 'round tank' 249cc BSA. By then I was earning 25 shillings a week, plus a small amount for playing the violin in a two-piece dance band on Saturday nights. So I could afford to pay my newly acquired machine off by instalments.

What a difference it made to my life to be able to get to that train in reasonable comfort. Not only that, but my new machine had quite a good carbide gas light. My push cycle had no light whatsoever, and I'd had to navigate that terrible pot-holey road in darkness.

So this is how my motorcycling days began. Not out of sport, or fun, but out of sheer necessity. However, I took every opportunity at public holiday times to tour the state as far as I could in the short time at my disposal.

At no time during my apprenticeship did the 'master', as he was designated in my indentures, ever speak to me. I saw him quite often but as far as he was concerned I never existed; yet I know full well he watched my progress carefully. At the end of my fourth year, after I passed my exams, I opened my pay packet and found they had paid me five shillings too much. I hastened after the boss's son to say there had been a mistake and the reply was, 'That's all right, son. You'll always get that now.'

It took me ages to find out why I had got that raise. Then it dawned on me that my college report was always forwarded on to the Master, and since my last report was favourable it was decreed that I should be paid an extra five shillings. I was then twenty years of age, and still lived in the same slab house.

My father died in an old men's home when I was eighteen. I never really knew him since his brain was affected by the two strokes and he was never cognisant of current affairs. Quite often he would ask what class I was in at school, even after I had been at work for almost two years. I never told anybody at work of my father's death, nor did I discuss my home life with anybody. I was a very sensitive child and kept skeletons in my own private cupboard.

At the age of twenty-two I finished my apprenticeship. What a relief that was. At long last I was a free agent. I no longer had a master, nor did I have to go to tech. I had finished with all that. I hankered for the wide open spaces, where I felt free and unfettered, and now I was able to move about the country as I wished, working here and there in interesting places.

After a few years I had saved enough money to seriously consider riding around Australia. It didn't take long to enlist a companion to join me in this venture. I was a close friend of the Smith family and Frank, the second eldest boy, who was a couple of years younger than me, elected to come too.

We planned the whole project together. Whatever time it would take us to complete the journey mattered little. It had never been done before and so long as we returned safely we would have established a record that no one else could claim. So we decided the whole thing would be done in a proper manner and under the supervision of the Auto Cycle Union of Australia. This body drew up a schedule of places around the continent including every capital city, not forgetting Darwin. The vast Northern Territory was at that time inhabited mainly by tribal Aborigines, with a few white settlers scattered sparsely over thousands of square miles managing and working on the large cattle stations. That itinerary also took us through the little-known far north of Western Australia. Our presence at each of the places listed had to be witnessed by a designated authority, to show that we really had arrived there by road. Hence our nightmare ride into Port Darwin, and out again on the same track—a distance of 400 miles which could have been covered in comfort on the railway train which ran weekly from Katherine to Darwin.

2

Getting Organised

IT WAS 1929, the year that marked the beginning of the Great Depression.

At that time motorists formed but a small percentage of the population and motoring beyond a 30-mile radius of Sydney was regarded more as a hazardous venture than anything else.

Roads were terrible; rough and full of pot-holes, covered with loose jagged metal. Further afield, they were as yet unmade. This, of course, only applied in the dry season and the time since the last road grading took place. The average motorist would consider a distance of 150 miles in any one day pretty good going. A day's journey without mishap was to be regarded as good motoring indeed.

Over a period of several years Frank Smith and I had become ardent motorcyclists and had toured far and wide over the state. We knew, therefore, that to complete a journey of over 9,000 miles in reasonably fast time would require something far above and beyond normal touring on so-called made roads in New South Wales. Luck was also to play a considerable part in a venture of this nature.

The Depression had begun to make its presence felt in industry and the various business houses associated with motoring were tightening up, so they turned a deaf ear to our approach for sponsorship. However, one or two firms were interested enough to at least give us some encouragement and arrange some form of welcome at the various cities we were to pass through. Maps were also arranged for us, although not all areas were mapped in those days, but we had to proceed to Brisbane before maps would be provided for the next leg— Brisbane to Darwin. The same procedure had to be carried out for the Darwin to Perth leg. We were to receive no financial support. But we had made up our minds anyhow, and decided we would foot the bill ourselves and make it a holiday.

We bought a brand new Magneto Model Harley-Davidson motorcycle and sidecar chassis for the standard price of £128. Being a Magneto Model, it was not fitted with a headlight— the standard headlight for this model being a carbide gas lamp. We chose a Magneto Model because battery-operated ignition for a venture of this magnitude was too hazardous. There would be no means of recharging a battery in the outlandish areas we were going.

There would be no white-overalled mechanics waiting for us every thousand miles or so, to take over and overhaul our machine. Nor were there blow-up beds, lightweight tents, transistor radios or bottled gas. We did not even have a watch. It was even doubtful if petrol would always be available.

It might seem strange that we elected to carry no headlights on a journey such as this. The reason is quite simple. Our trip was not a test of speed and we decided not to travel at night. I had once before become lost through travelling at night, even though conditions had seemed favourable. But to become lost in the north of Australia's great waterless uninhabited regions would be another matter altogether. It was safer to stay put after dark in areas such as these. Hence no lights.

The north of Australia was virtually unknown. Few people had been there, and fewer people lived there. Communications were all but non-existent. Radio was not yet widely used, air services were in their infancy and Qantas terminated its once-a-week flight at Camooweal. Beyond there lay the vast open spaces of northern Australia. Contact with the rest of the world would cease until the Overland Telegraph Line could be contacted, some thousand miles to the north. Even then this form of communication would be short-lived, as the telegraph line would coincide only with about 300 miles of our total journey. There was still the rest of the great north-west to traverse, along the 'Madman's Track' and through the Kimberleys, until

15

we would contact the telegraph line linking Broome with Perth.

There were to be weeks and weeks when we would be unheard of, and it was only when we reached points of communication such as Darwin and Broome that we could reassure our friends and family that we were still alive.

The Aborigines of the Northern Territory and the Kimberleys were nomadic, and few of them had even a passing acquaintance with Western civilisation. In fact, few had ever seen a white man and in those days it was not uncommon for a whole tribe to be brought into Darwin for a murder trial, the males chained to each other and herded along by a white mounted policeman and his assistant blacktrackers. Spearings of natives and of white men were not yet a thing of the past.

So with these thoughts in mind, we commenced to get our things together and provide ways and means of carrying additional petrol for long distances between pick-up points. We also had to make up, and fit, special water tanks, and compile a list of necessary spares.

Having paid our money and now being the joint-owners of this new and highly polished piece of machinery, it was time for preparation in earnest. But first of all we had to ride the outfit from Bennett & Wood in William Street through the busy city to the preparation site. This venture almost turned out to be a rather bad start in itself, for we had not travelled three miles before an observant mounted police officer noted we did not have a rear numberplate. We received a please explain notice.

It was customary for the vendors of motorcycles to register a machine before passing it over to the purchaser, so he could legally take it on to the highway. A numberplate was supplied by the authorities and was attached to the front mudguard. However, it had recently become necessary to affix a similar plate to the rear mudguard, but this second plate was the responsibility of the owner.

This was indeed a great start for such an ambitious venture as ours, but we got the additional plate and heard nothing

Frank Smith, left, and Jack Bowers fitted
out in new clothes and ready to depart

Setting out from Sydney GPO, 4 July 1929

The 'road' near Cloncurry

Frank bags a
kangaroo

Dinner near the
Barcoo River, central
Queensland

Food for a day or
two at Camooweal

Aborigines' camp at
No. 2 Bore,
Northern Territory

General overhaul at
No. 19 Bore, Alexan-
dria cattle station,
Northern Territory

more from the authorities governing such things as number-plates and the duplication thereof.

In the meantime, we had plenty to do in organising our equipment.

On our previous trips Frank and I had used a coffin-like box attached to a motorcycle in lieu of the more comfortable and upholstered standard sidecar, mainly because a box-like structure carried more gear, could not be easily scratched or dented, and was made of much sturdier material. Seeing no reason to stray from this practice, we constructed our box accordingly, with one or two small variations. The box was of one-inch solid planking, fastened with screws at the joints, and the bottom section was made to extend fifteen inches beyond the rest of the woodwork, providing a shelf on which could be bolted the extra petrol container, which was in reality an eight-gallon tank used in the Ford T Model motor cars of the day. A seat was installed a few inches above the baseboard, upon which would rest a circular inflatable rubber cushion. The box was kept narrow enough for spare tyres to be secured on either end with a minimum of lashings, but was wide enough to allow the passenger some comfort. The two end sections were partitioned off to stow essential spares and commodities. Unobtrusive brackets were screwed on either side, one for the shotgun and the other for the heavy repeating rifle, which could then be brought into action at short notice. We knew our skill as marksmen could mean the difference between a meal and starvation, and also took with us a Browning automatic pistol.

Stout mild steel brackets were also made to straddle the standard luggage rack over the rear mudguard. These brackets had to carry two two-gallon water tanks, one for each side, over which a piece of board was bolted to keep them in position. It also provided a flat base upon which our five blankets and tent fly, rolled in the form of a swag, were securely strapped. The water tanks were standard cans, in 24-gauge galvanised iron outer jackets. It was as well we provided this added strength to the cans since, due to the continual sloshing of the water,

17

they became leaky long before we had completed our trip. There was always a little bit of water imprisoned between the inner and the outer jackets. No taps were affixed to the spare fuel tank or the water cans, as they could be inadvertently left partly open or even be knocked into an open position. The only means of extracting petrol or water was by syphoning it with a rubber tube.

Water in some areas we would have to cover would be a matter of life or death, and fuel could well play as prominent a part in survival. As it turned out, almost every time we had a breakdown or were compelled to stop for some unforeseen reason we were out of water. This was partly brought about due to the extra weight burdening the luggage carrier and partly because water was not always available when the tanks became empty. At most times our only way of washing our faces free of dust was with two or three capfuls syphoned off into a small bowl, or by cupping our hands and sloshing water over our faces.

Finally the day arrived for our departure. It was 4 July 1929, but dates would matter less than distances in the months that followed. With £60 cash in the money belt our sole financial resource, we drove into the Harley agency in Sydney before the final departure.

As we drove out the salesroom doorway we had to negotiate the street gutter and the sidecar flew so high into the air the sales manager who observed this violent upward flight probably wondered if it was rocket-powered. He frantically waved us to return and suggested we fit an extra leaf in each of the elliptical springs to lessen this tremendous bounce. It was not until we were fully loaded that such a severe bouncing motion was fully apparent and we were to be very thankful that those extra springs had been fitted when we came upon particularly atrocious tracks.

As it was, we seemed to spend most of our time riding one-handed, with the right hand manipulating the twist grip throttle and the left held ready to repel any violent upward tendency in the sidebox. We became expert at quickly clutching at the side of the box, not only to prevent too much upward movement, but also to assist in lowering it, thus helping reduce the strain on the sidecar chassis. Despite these efforts, however, the chassis finally did fracture.

But then so did many other things as well.

3

The Adventure Begins

WE LEFT SYDNEY in mid-winter because we had been advised to pass through the north of Australia well before the wet season set in. During 'the wet' rivers that were sand beds for most of the year become raging torrents and utterly impassable.

So with many good wishes, much hand-shaking and farewells generally, we were off. The official departure took place at 1 p.m. on 4 July, outside the Sydney GPO. What lay before us and when, or if, we would return was anybody's guess.

July is a cold month and the prospect of camping for the night without shelter was a far from enviable one. We looked forward to the warmer conditions in the north, but it was to be many weeks before we were warm enough to shed our heavy riding apparel, of which we were immensely proud anyway.

At the end of the first day's run, when darkness forced us to a halt, the camping spot was far from good but there was enough room at the side of the road to light a fire and put the billy on. Selecting two stout sticks, we poked them through sections of the outfit to support the tent fly. This structure resembled a large dog kennel, into which we crawled. Here we spread our five blankets on a groundsheet and prepared to spend the night. Sleep under these conditions on a cold night is not easy, but this was to be our only form of shelter for the next eleven weeks and in all climates, except for those very few nights we spent in cities or in homesteads.

By our first nightfall we had only covered 73 miles. Seventy-three miles in four hours; an average of 18 miles per hour. Of those miles the first 30 were within the metropolitan area and for the most part on good bitumen. The remaining 43 miles were rough, pot-holey, and through the mountainous country of the MacDonald Ranges. From now on we could not expect much better conditions.

The main route from Sydney to Brisbane followed a different course from that of today, and ran through the old historic towns of Parramatta, Windsor, Cattai and Wisemans Ferry, where we crossed the Hawkesbury by vehicular ferry. From here on the rough metal road wended its way up and over the MacDonald Ranges.

A small ferry—propelled by hand—provided the necessary crossing over the MacDonald River at St Albans. Further on lay the sleepy little village of Wollombi and the larger towns of Cessnock and Singleton. From there the route followed that of the present New England Highway but the road surface continued rough and pot-holed for most of the way to the New England town of Tenterfield. After that the road was an unmade dirt one crossing the MacPherson Range at Spicers Gap, where roadwork excavation was in progress and made the going almost impossible. It was here that we were to cross the border of New South Wales into Queensland.

As we climbed into the higher altitudes of the New England ranges, the cold intensified and snow drifts lay on the sides of the road. We made certain that our camping spot was in a well-timbered area, where firewood was readily available, and near a stream.

We would stretch the tent fly over two sticks thrust horizontally into open sections of the bike framework to carry the canvas canopy as scant protection from the elements. Then, spreading our groundsheet and blankets on the bare ground, we prepared our lowly couch for a cold night's sleep.

During one night we were rudely awakened by some unknown furry animal obviously intent upon sharing the meagre warmth of our five thin blankets.

At moments such as these man's nervous system reacts with great alacrity. Every muscle is quickly summoned to respond to the danger. Vocal cords loudly and agitatedly demand 'What the hell!' There is kicking of legs and waving of arms. Our

21

frantic endeavours to repel all intruders caused great havoc within such a confined space. We could not stand erect in a defensive position, nor could we escape to the wide open spaces. So we fought off this intruder in a more or less recumbent position with much kicking, shouts of alarm and unseemly language. Could it be a snake? No, it had fur, but then all furry creatures have teeth, and a nasty habit of biting first and thinking later. In the event, our panicky violent actions were such that our intruder sought instant escape.

Had we pondered more fully upon this midnight interlude we might have welcomed our furry visitor into our midst. As a boy I remember reading a story entitled 'The Man and the Wolf'. In it, the man and wolf combined warmth by huddling together. That cold night all three of us could have likewise huddled together and shared our bodily warmth.

However, we gave that thought no room in our frantic state of mind, and the small bush animal got a much hotter reception than the coldness of our camp spot warranted.

Each morning in this region, when we had escaped our cold blankets at the crack of dawn, we'd lose no time in kicking the overnight embers together and adding more fuel to our camp fire. Then, when our sluggish circulation had reached a point of reasonable comfort, one of us would take the billy across the frosty crackling ground and down to the creek. Each day began with a mug of tea.

The morning after we'd fought off our intruder, however, it was not just a case of dipping the billy into a stream of bubbling water. Overnight, the stream had ceased to bubble. It just lay there, doggo, a silent sheet of glassy, challenging ice. We broke the surface hurriedly, dipped the billy in and scurried back to the man-made warmth of our camp fire where we stood and rotated as if on a rotisserie until bodily warmth was restored.

I usually took the morning shift at the handlebars and rode until midday, or until a suitable lunchtime spot appealed. Therefore I mounted to the cold saddle and, wearing a pair of spare woollen socks over my gauntleted hands, took to the road. It was sheer torture to sit there without bodily activity but I steeled myself against the cold by clamping my teeth tightly together and wearing a grim and determined look. And as the speedo crept slowly towards the ten-mile mark I decided that, come what may, I would stop when the number 10 appeared. The moment it did so I clamped the footbrake in the 'on' position and sprang from my seat. Heavily encumbered as I was, I started running, as if to abandon the outfit and finish the journey on foot. In this I was quickly followed by Frank, whose idea seemed identical with mine. After about 200 yards we turned and retraced our steps to our outfit, resumed our positions and carried on.

For the next two weeks this morning procedure became the regular one. Watching that sluggish speedo slowly climb from the zero setting to 10 was sheer agony. My toes and fingers would be numb with the cold. But at no time was I prepared to undertake that morning jog before the magic figure appeared. My eyes were focused on the speedo perhaps more than on the hazardous road.

The sun warmed up within an hour or two and we would then stop for morning tea. We carefully rationed a shortbread cake which had been given to us by a motherly well-wisher at our departure. At lunch time it became Frank's turn to take over while I sat back in the sidebox and admired the scenery. This became our general pattern throughout, except that the shortbread quickly disappeared from the routine. Shortages and sharing, not to mention a sense of humour, were our allies for that gruelling trip, and beyond.

We had tried to supplement our slender purse by finding some likely sponsor such as oil companies or the Harley-Davidson Sydney agents. But as the world was just beginning to enter into a universal depression all the companies we approached regretted they were unable to use our exploit as an advertising medium. The Harley-Davidson people did, however, give us a sweater each.

Unbeknown to us, the managers of the companies that

denied us sponsorship were also quite aware of the human dangers in this type of venture. Men who had started out quite good friends would finish as enemies: hardship, unsavoury conditions, breakdowns and other factors would be their undoing, plus the well-known fact that isolation can lead to strange fancies. Constant living in close contact can often lead to quarrels which commence as minor ones but become magnified to such an extent that close friendships of many years standing break down and bring down the whole project.

Frank and I had been friends since our schooldays—when he was twelve and I fourteen. By the time we were well into our teens we had become ardent motorcyclists and, with his older brother Alan, we ventured far afield at every opportunity to view little known and remote areas of New South Wales.

These were arduous trips, with long hours of hard riding along rarely used mountain tracks; bouncing up and down over those rugged trails, each with a heavy pack on his back and pausing only for our morning billy of tea and our meagre midday meal. This was our early training.

And just to show those doubting Thomases our ability to refrain from becoming deadly enemies, we returned to Sydney still friends after our gruelling ride around the continent, later married two sisters, each raised a small family, and remained partners in business for over half a century.

Seven days after our departure from Sydney GPO we triumphantly arrived in Brisbane, where we were welcomed by various representatives of oil companies, tyre companies and the Harley-Davidson agents for that city. So far we had had no trouble with our outfit whatever. The motor had not missed a beat, nor had we had even one puncture. This was to be regarded as good motoring, but we still had a long long way to go before we re-entered Sydney from the South. What lay ahead of us in those intervening 9,000 miles we knew not.

4

Mud and Prickly Pear

WE LEFT BRISBANE after a two-day stay and after passing through Toowoomba entered the south-western area of Queensland. This was dairying country of black soil, fairly well timbered but infested with acre upon acre of prickly pear. This introduced cactus, which had already reached pest proportions, was being slowly but firmly eradicated in some areas by the introduction of the *Cactoblastis* moth.

We awoke one morning and found a light shower of rain had fallen during the night. This caused us no undue concern. Our canvas lean-to had kept us dry as we slept.

However, there had been just enough rain to turn the heavy black soil into a sticky mud, and when the engine refused to answer the throttle we dismounted to investigate. Mud had built up between the front wheel and the mudguard to such an extent it had a braking effect. Coming to a patch of sand we stupidly thought this would help to cut away the mud. The tyre had worn down quite considerably by the time the smell of burning rubber dispelled this thought. This we could not afford, so we finally had no alternative to laboriously raking out the mud with a screwdriver. A few hundred yards further on we had to repeat the same process. The morning wore on and on in this fashion. We were getting nowhere. Fortunately the sun broke through the clouds, the mud dried quickly and once again we could make good steady progress.

These black soil tracks, once dry, were far better for travel than the so-called made roads. Our tyres and our machine generally were not subjected to the terrific beating they got from the jagged, and pot-holey roads that then connected the capital cities.

Prickly pear walled both sides of the track for mile after mile, and towards nightfall we still could not find an opening in this wall of cactus to enable us to leave the narrow track to make camp for the night.

We rode on in the gathering darkness for another sixteen miles before we at last found an opening leading to a small clearing. An excellent camping spot at long last. We hastily commenced gathering firewood since the nights were still bitterly cold. As we wandered farther afield we suddenly came upon a tombstone. Then we found another, and yet another. We were camped in an old cemetery—unused, and neglected. Headstones were dotted here and there amongst the prickly pear and scant timber.

However, it was not the departed spirits that caused us worry during the night. It was the numbers of scorpions darting out of the burning logs of our camp fire and disappearing hurriedly in every direction to escape the searing heat.

We were so thankful that we had located an open camping spot before darkness fell that we had not even thought about other creatures also occupying this lonely graveyard. Still, we had no alternative but to remain and deal with the situation as best we could. We had no camp stretchers and were obliged to sleep on the bare ground with but a groundsheet and one blanket upon which to rest. Lying there watching those venomous creatures hurrying towards us in an endeavour to escape the blazing logs was not a pleasant prelude to settling down to sleep.

Resourcefulness being a necessity in cases such as these, it was not long before we decided to build another fire of lesser heat between the main one and our sleeping area. That should distract the unsavoury residents of these tinder-dry, half-rotting logs and persuade them to seek refuge in places other than our blankets and vulnerable bodies.

Thus encouraged, we turned in and slept until morning. Sheer expediency was rapidly teaching us some of the lesser but important skills of bushcraft.

The following day we learned from the locals that this area

was regarded as the most vermin-infested part of Australia. The vermin were provided excellent protection by the cactus.

The locals also recounted for our benefit the story of some drovers who, like us, could find nowhere to leave the track. Eventually they camped in the same old cemetery where they, too, quickly became aware of the vast numbers of scorpions escaping the heat of their camp fire. The drovers began to spread out in alarm and as they backed away from the fire each man was intent on scanning the ground for wayward scorpions bearing down on them. One wag, apparently not so timid as his companions, plucked a thorn from a nearby cactus and jabbed it into the bare leg of his nearest neighbour. The yell that rent the air of that otherwise quiet night was still being enjoyed by the townsfolk of Chinchilla.

Day after day from sunup to sundown we battled on, and we were well into western Queensland before we had our first puncture. We had travelled 1,500 miles since leaving Sydney, had averaged 100 miles a day and were long overdue for tyre trouble. Under the prevailing conditions, tyres and tubes take a heavy toll from the pounding of projecting rocks and jagged pot-holes. If we pumped the tyres up harder, the pounding was taken up by the back wheel, so spokes would loosen or break. If we deflated the tyres the inner tube would suffer, as projecting rocks would flex the tyre inwards and break the canvas wall casings. This break would then slowly but surely rip away at the inner tube until a slow leak would leave us with a flat tyre. We therefore had to try and strike a happy medium between reduced tyre pressure and broken spokes. In the rocky mineral-bearing area near Cloncurry huge stones in the track were impossible to avoid. Tyres and wheels, and in fact the whole framework of our machine and sidecar, took severe punishment.

Between Cloncurry and Mount Isa the track was covered with a layer of dust several inches thick. It was my turn in the saddle and I was too busy watching where I was going to glance at Frank, but when I finally did so, to see how he was taking it, I nearly laughed in his face. He was unrecognisable. Dust enshrouded him from head to foot and he peered up at me through his goggles, presenting a most ludicrous sight. I was bad enough, but had the advantage of riding higher above the road surface. As usual, water was at a premium but at camp that night we spared enough to fill our cupped hands and at least wash the front of our faces. Sufficient anyway to enable us to sleep for the night in reasonable comfort.

By this time our meals had downgraded to minimal standards. Self-raising flour was now left back in the more progressive towns. Bread was in a similar category. All we had was plain flour, to which we added baking powder to make it rise, and water. Puftaloons and flapjacks appeared on the menu, together with jam and tea. Jam ultimately gave way to treacle, for the flies disputed ownership of the jam with its open lid, whereas the knock-on lid of the treacle tin foiled them entirely, and so a menu was evolved due to dire necessity.

Mount Isa at that time comprised a straggly row of tents and shanties bordering either side of this horrible dry and dusty track. We did not even pause, but rode on to select a less arid and dusty camp site. It was a further 162 miles to the next town—Camooweal—and the only thing shown on our map over this distance was a waterhole located about midway between Cloncurry and Camooweal.

About this time our crankcase began to leak oil so badly that we each had one jackboot saturated with it. The motor became so hot as to be almost unbearable on the right leg and the rider would constantly change resting places on the footboard to avoid the heat. We also found one of the stays on our water tank carrier had broken, causing a persistent and annoying rattle. Our outfit had started to crack up at 1,800 miles with still about 8,000 to go. We too were beginning to show signs of wear and tear. Frank's leather breeches had already started to give way. Only the outer leg seams alone remained intact, so the breeches were secured around his waist by his leather belt and tucked into the tops of the lace-up jackboots. At least there was no fear that his pants would part company with his person while he has in a sitting position.

However, Frank must have come from a long line of English huntsmen for he had a hunting instinct which came to the fore upon sight of almost anything landborne in fur or feathers. So upon our first close-up view of an emu standing sedately viewing our noisy approach, Frank suddenly swerved from the track and took up the chase around stumps, dodging trees, bounding over the uneven terrain in hot pursuit of this long-legged bird who was capable of clocking up 30 mph. In the meantime, I was being hurled into the air by the bounding coffin-like sidebox and then rocked hard back into my seat on the blow-up cushion. I could only clutch onto the side of the box in wonderment and hope for the best.

Upon my carefully worded reproach Frank agreed to desist from this kind of hunting. As I pointed out, we had many many miles yet to go. He thereupon decided to mend his ways and to chase his quarry on foot. On occasion he would suddenly propel himself from saddle or sidebox and give chase to a small kangaroo joey with his breeches flapping wildly in the wind of his momentum. He apparently had great faith in his leather belt, but being hopelessly out of running form he presented a most astounding figure somewhat resembling a large Afghan hound with flailing arms, heavy jackboots, and bobbing pompom bouncing precariously atop his neatly folded balaclava cap. I would sit back and watch this amusing spectacle, take advantage of the brief respite and relax.

Joeys have remarkable powers of acceleration, and upon seeing itself being pursued by such a strange apparition the joey would head for a slight uphill incline and, about halfway up, put its foot down, as it were, and accelerate. Meanwhile Frank would labour to the summit in second gear and both would temporarily disappear down the far slope. The last thing I would see would be the bobbing pompom on Frank's balaclava. It would not be long, I knew, before the pompom would make its appearance once more, this time in a more stable condition as Frank slowly and meditatively made his way back to the outfit. He would then take up his former position and resume the endeavour to circumnavigate the continent. He never did tell me what he was going to do with a joey if he managed to catch one, or with an emu for that matter. We had no room for either in the sidebox.

I think it was his hunting instinct that precipitated the ultimate breakdown of Frank's leather riding breeches, for every strenuous step he took in pursuit of a joey took its toll of the remaining cotton thread holding them together.

Apart from our leather breeches we each owned, with great pride and joy, a beautiful brown riding coat. Double-breasted, made of three layers of light canvas and two layers of rubber, belted at the waist, and with a high, button-up collar. We continually reminded each other what good tough coats they were and, to use a favourite saying in reference to their toughness, 'We could climb through a barbed-wire fence in them'.

One day I found myself reclining in the sidebox after having finished my half-day in the saddle. I gazed out over the surrounding countryside and ruminated on our general progress. Without warning the ever-bounding sidebox, projected into the air by a slightly heavier bump than usual, hurled me skywards out of synchronisation with the heavy iron bracket holding the near-side water tank. As I went up, so the bracket came down, missing my reclining arm by a hair's breadth but cunningly managing to collect the sleeve of my beautiful riding coat. There was a ripping sound and, on inspection, a three-inch tear right through the five layers of canvas and rubber. Frank took time off to see what made that sound and burst into such uncontrollable laughter he almost fell out of the saddle.

I thought this conduct most unseemly. There was nothing in this unfortunate accident to warrant such mirth and in true Australian spirit I simply said, 'Silly bastard'. This remark only led to further merriment on Frank's part, but he regained his equilibrium on the saddle and continued on his way, leaving me to sit back on my blow-up cushion trying not to examine the damage to my sleeve. I could hardly believe that the sidecar and iron bracket could have rendered me such a cruel blow. When I looked up at Frank again I saw tears running down his cheeks and I was in no way uncertain about their cause.

He wasn't crying because he was upset that I had torn my coat, nor was he in any way put out about my calling him a silly bastard.

Two days later I was in the saddle and Frank was in the sidebox when, yet again, up went the sidebox and down came the carrier bracket. Frank's right sleeve was ripped in exactly the same place as mine had been. My tears were not those of mortification.

We treated both coat sleeves in similar fashion, by cutting a piece of white adhesive tape from our medicine box and taping up each tear. We hoped these identical pieces of white tape on a brown background might be regarded by interested spectators as being some badge of distinction issued only to 'Around Australia' motorcyclists.

Being able to laugh at our misfortunes was of great importance to our venture and reflected well on our general attitude. In what might appear to be almost a matter of life and death, such as when the engine gave out a hundred miles from nowhere, we would both dismount, walk gingerly around our machine and look terribly worried. Then, seeing the worried and anxious look on each other's faces, we would both break into laughter. After that we would just as seriously set about finding ways and means of rectifying the trouble. Somehow or other we were always triumphant.

And if there was any weakness anywhere in our outfit we most certainly found it and fixed it. We used pieces of fencing wire for this and that, bolts and plates for the cracked front forks, and even borrowed a blacksmith's forge and anvil to repair the cracked sidecar chassis.

The continual pounding over rocks and gibbers took great toll of the back wheel and at sundown, when we had called it a day, we would go over the spokes to see how many were broken or required additional tension; sometimes we would discover a slow leak and we had as many as seven sleeves in the back tyre at the one time. After locating a slow leak and repairing it we would then have to laboriously hold each sleeve in its proper position before replacing the outer casing.

It was well that we could afford to laugh, given these varying and numerous troubles.

By the time we arrived in Perth, we had a patchwork bike. The water tank carrier was wired down with No. 8 fencing wire tensioned to great effect with a Cobb & Co. hitch taught us by an old stockman at a large cattle station in the far north. He had also provided the wire. Our front forks had cracked and were braced with a stout mild steel plate held in position on either side of the fracture with 5/16-inch 'U' bolts. We had an improvised bracket similarly supporting a fracture in the castings of the sidecar chassis. This we had made using the facilities of the blacksmith's shop at Moora-Boola Aboriginal station, also in the far north.

The inner lining jackets of both water tanks had also become leaky. But our foresight in providing the tanks with outer casings luckily prevented any loss of their precious contents.

We had also thrown two tyres away, due to cuts made by sharp stones, and by then possessed no further spares. The passenger's blow-up cushion in the sidebox also bore a patch covering a leak caused by friction with the baseboard. The overhanging baseboard of the sidebox itself had been shortened by six inches due to constant impact with the ground when negotiating steep and narrow gullies and creek crossings.

These are just some of the running repairs we had to carry out en route. Fortunately, however, we had no real trouble with the 7–9 horsepower Harley vee-twin engine. Despite the rough treatment it had received, with the occasional and necessary usage of windmill oil for lubrication, the greatest problem was the oiling up of the magneto in some isolated location or another. However from time to time, we took time out to completely dismantle the engine, scrape the carbon from the pistons and cylinder heads, grind in the inlet and exhaust valves and adjust valve tappets. This usually took us two days and we always reserved this chore until we arrived at a camping site where we would not be beset by a crowd of curious and inquisitive onlookers who might hinder our progress. On these overhauls each of us had his own side of the machine to work on, when it came to removing the engine from the frame.

As we bounded over the awful rock-strewn track on our way to Cloncurry at a speed of five or six miles an hour, there, high overhead, flying steadily towards the same destination, was the Qantas mail plane. Cloncurry would be its most northerly objective. Here it would unload the mail and then retrace its flightpath back south to Brisbane. Qantas has indeed enlarged its horizon since those days. But here we were, battling and struggling, fighting the terrain every inch of the way to Cloncurry, and hoping letters for us had been dropped off there. The pilot would be there in a few hours, and in comfort, while the same distance would take us days in the utmost discomfort.

And when we did finally arrive, there was no mail for us. It was said we were travelling too fast! Two months later we collected those letters away on the far side of the continent in the little Western Australian pearling town of Broome. The return stamps stretched across each envelope from one side to the other. They did eventually arrive by Qantas at Cloncurry, and were then forwarded to Camooweal, but we were always one or two days ahead, so back they went by Qantas to Brisbane, and then back to Sydney. They then travelled across the Nullabor Plain by mail train to Perth and from there over 1,000 miles north by the slow Western Australian rail system to Meekatharra. Here the railway terminated, so they continued on to the more northerly port of Broome by whatever means of conveyance was available. So even in those days the mail still got through. Apparently it was just a matter of time.

Midway between Mount Isa and Camooweal was a waterhole marked and we decided that would be our next goal.

Having arrived at this spot we discovered a bark shanty occupied by a lone dingo trapper who welcomed us wholeheartedly. And here over a most welcome meal, prepared by our new friend, we spent the next two hours just eating and yarning. We learned quite a lot from the old trapper—in particular how to make a damper and how to make a bushman's brownie, which was what we were eating at the time. We also learnt that we had to add cream of tartar and baking soda to plain flour to make it rise. It was either two of cream of tartar to one of soda or vice versa—we never could remember which—but we made out all right in the long run.

Camooweal was the last township we would see for many hundreds of miles. Six miles north of here we would cross from Queensland into the Northern Territory. The only towns between here and Port Darwin were few, far between, and of little consequence.

Since bidding the dingo trapper farewell our real troubles had started. Sixty miles did not seem far and we should have been in Camooweal by nightfall, but the petrol gave out nine miles from town. The water cans were also empty, and we had no food except for nine galahs—those squawking, screeching, pink and grey parrots found in large gregarious flocks in the Outback. As a last resource they can be boiled and eaten, but any Australian bushman will tell you to boil them with an old boot and when the boot is tender the galahs are cooked!

So here we were, with no petrol, no food, a nine-mile walk into Camooweal for petrol, and of course nine-mile walk back again. Frank elected to walk into town while I remained in case someone who could spare a quart, or even a pint of petrol chanced to pass by. I did not hold out much hope for a passer-by since we hadn't seen anybody other than the dingo trapper since leaving Mount Isa the previous day.

Just about sunset I sighted four or five horses walking in single file through the scattered timber, and I knew that they were headed for water. I also knew that horses will stand and gaze at man for interminable periods so, keeping out of sight and dodging from tree to tree, I began to follow them. But the thought that I might miss a passing motorist caused me to forget my thirst and return to the outfit.

Towards nightfall I gathered enough dry wood to keep a fire going all night so Frank would not pass right by, for this country bears no distinguishing marks and preserves a monotonous sameness.

As Frank trudged back along the track carrying a can of petrol, darkness had long since fallen on the lonely silent track.

34

He was alone with his thoughts, with no road signs to guide him or mile pegs to indicate distance and, having no watch, he could only guess at his progress. His thoughts turned to the prospect of actually passing the campsite. If I fell asleep it only needed the camp fire to go out for the whole scene to merge into the surroundings. But at long last he saw my distant fire. As he sat on the petrol can, thirsty and tired, he cogitated on his fate. An eighteen-mile walk, practically non-stop, weighed down for half of it with a gallon of petrol is no mean feat, especially for someone who had been sitting down on a motor-cycle or resting in the sidebox all day and every day for the past three weeks. His only other exercise had been the occasional foot race after joeys.

He had called at the pub in Camooweal, mainly to see if anyone was coming back our way and could give him a lift. He had figured that whoever came along that lonely, thirsty track would almost certainly make the pub his last call. His luck was out, and after paying two shillings for his beer he commenced his return journey. That the same beer in Sydney would have cost sevenpence.

Frank had brought no water with him, and the walk and the beer had made him thirsty. So was I, but there it was. At last we had petrol, and with only nine miles to go to town we turned in for a few hours sleep.

We were up at first light and on our way, but luck was still against us. Before we had gone three miles, the sidecar tyre punctured. Still, it was a simple enough matter to repair the puncture and at long last we came upon the town's water reservoir. Here we quenched our thirst, had a much-needed wash and saw to it that our water tanks were filled to the brim. Then finally we rode into the little border town of Camooweal.

5

Bush Tucker

APART FROM our riding jackets and leather breeches we each possessed a woollen sweater of which we were inordinately proud. These had been a gift from the Harley-Davidson people—the only gift we had received from anyone in the motoring world. The sweaters were a brilliant orange and sewn across the chest and back, in large black letters, were the words Harley-Davidson. They were further enhanced by black crewneck collars and cuffs. We proudly thought these sweaters would be highly successful in attracting the opposite sex, but had had no chance to put our theory to the test. There was little that was elegant about our other clothes and Frank's riding breeches were literally falling apart at the seams.

Man is a proud, noble creature. Rob him of his nether garments by one means or another and he quickly becomes an introvert. All his once-proud bearing begins to disappear, he shuns society and his entire outlook in life becomes narrow and worthless. Such was Frank's fate as he rode throughout the day depending solely on his belt and his jackboots to keep his pants on. Fortunately his khaki shorts gave some form of protection from insect bites.

It was in this dishevelled condition that we presented ourselves to the Camooweal saddler. Here could well have been the terminating point in the whole venture, for no man can really be expected to break motoring records without his pants, but it was the saddler's wife who came to our rescue and helped Frank out of his trouble.

The saddler obviously knew horses and their requirements well, but when it came to fancy leather trousers for men his mind appeared to boggle. Perhaps he had thoughts of his drinking mates seeing him repairing with delicate fingers a pair of men's trousers instead of manfully handling a buckjumping saddle, or a stock saddle. Whatever his thoughts were on this subject, he summoned his wife and handed us over to her safe-keeping, washing his hands of the whole business. She quickly took over and, removing Frank's pants, departed to some inner sanctum to effect repairs.

Frank meanwhile stood and waited wearing his 'other' pants. Fortunately we each carried a separate pair of 'dress' pants for special occasions, as required by society from time to time. Some little time later the saddler's wife appeared with the treasured garment repaired with stout cotton and Frank, evidently no longer given to chasing the wildlife of Australia on foot, had no further trouble with his breeches.

However, there was still the matter of payment to be arrived at. Shifting uneasily from foot to foot, Frank made the opening remark of negotiation by hesitantly asking 'How much?' The saddler's wife, equally hesitant, and also moving from foot to foot in an uncertain manner, shyly said, 'Oh, we'll leave that to you'.

Hello, I thought, they've reached a stalemate.

'No,' said Frank, 'I'll leave it to you.'

And so they became deadlocked. Frank finally ended the impasse by adopting a benevolent and magnaminimous bearing, thrusting his hand deep into his trouser pocket and producing a two-shilling piece which he thrust into the work-worn palm of his benefactress. Before any further negotiations could be entered into we took our departure.

Having been restored to the social strata of life, Frank became quite jaunty once more. The fact that two shillings was exactly the price of one glass of beer in Camooweal in no way disconcerted him. Now, wearing his newly repaired breeches, he could once more hold his head on high.

At Camooweal we also discovered that we were beyond the realm of both bread and baking powder. Maybe bread was sometimes available, but no, not even baking powder, and from this point on it was flour plus cream of tartar and soda—two of one and one of the other—or starve.

As we slowly left civilisation behind us we were pretty well on our own, and this fact was revealed to us in no uncertain manner as we found ourselves reduced to living standards similar to those of the local Aborigines. The next meal would probably depend upon our skill with the rifle, though if game was not available we still had our remaining flour, cream of tartar, soda and water. Suet also proved to be an excellent additive to the flour and water. That is when we had any. Dripping, or animal fat, would have also served the purpose, but climatic conditions were not favourable to carrying it for long periods.

On occasions when we had no suet, we flattened the flour-and-water dough to cover the bottom of the frying pan like a pancake, and fried it very slowly over a low fire. The result looked like a bread board which we cut fair across the middle. Half each, no more, and no less. Spread with treacle it made quite a good substitute for bread and became our regular breakfast meal.

Frank is a bigger, better, and faster eater than I am. Seated on his favourite meal-time seat, the flour tin, he would ravenously devour his half pancake with obvious relish, then sit back silently like a hungry dog, watching me as I slowly ate mine. However, I could not afford to yield a crumb.

Another dish which regularly appeared on the menu, also of flour and water, with a little suet added, was mixed and rolled into little balls, like a golf ball. These would be boiled in the billy until they became almost as large as tennis balls. The billy-can could only hold two. Boiled for twenty minutes, then spread with treacle, they would be our one hot meal of the day. Almost like dessert.

This was our standard bill of fare for the next three months. Occasionally it was varied by turkey, wild duck or galahs, depending upon what popped up during the day. Kangaroos and walleroos—a larger species of kangaroo—were plentiful but we lacked the time to skin and prepare kangaroo steaks.

Bush turkeys were the favourite dish. These large birds were generally found in pairs. Being heavy, they require a long runway before lift-off, and it was at this stage they would fall prey to our rifle or shotgun. The man in the sidebox could rest the rifle on the edge of the box and take the bird on the left— a sitting shot—and the rider in the saddle, using the shotgun, would bring down the other bird before it became airborne.

Both of us would quickly vault from our seats and, armed with a tomahawk or an Aborigine's throwing stick, would take off in hot pursuit if the birds were only winged. We would generally return with a bird each. Without wasting any further time, we would cut the legs and breasts from each bird and stow them away in the meat tin which held sufficient for the next two days. These savoury morsels would be fried in a little suet, just like steaks. Due to the wholesale slaughter of these birds in subsequent years, bush turkeys are now a protected species.

6

Not a Tree in Sight

THE TIMBERED COUNTRY had begun to peter out near
Camooweal, and we were now on the verge of the Barkly
Tableland. We had said goodbye to railways, postal services
and telephones. Letters posted after our departure had not
caught up with us and the newspapers were all back issues.
Still, we read all about our departure from Brisbane in the
papers flown into Camooweal on the Qantas plane which
arrived the same day we did.

The going became much better after leaving Camooweal.
The country was dead flat and the surface of the dirt track so
even, wide and smooth that we could choose our own track.
We preferred, however, to keep some wheelmarks in sight to
keep on a straight course across the dusty, barren plain. As we
raced along in these favourable conditions, trees became an
increasing rarity until finally, on the great Ranken Plain, we
turned and watched the last one disappear over the horizon
behind us. We stopped, dismounted and looked around us.
Here was a vast flat expanse of country. It was the first time
in my life that I had been unable to see a tree within such a
large field of vision.

Towards late afternoon we entered lightly timbered country
once again and arrived at No. 19 bore. A pumping station
directing artesian water into a long line of drinking troughs for
stock being driven overland to markets in the south was the
only sign of habitation. It was time to take stock of our situation.

Our map was a blueprint about three feet long and showed a
white line from bottom to top, upon which were marked the
various cattle stations through which we would pass as we

Roadside repairs,
northern Australia

Eagle with six-foot
wingspan, central
Australia

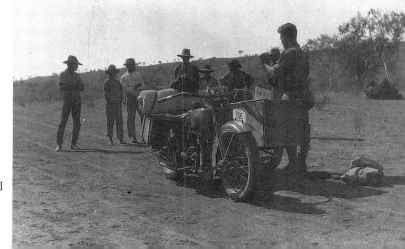

Interested Aboriginal
stockmen, northern
Australia

Katherine to Darwin road by the Overland Telegraph, then and now

travelled north-west towards Katherine and Darwin. We would have to trust to the hospitality of these places for petrol, flour and other necessary commodities. All these large stations carried a store for station use and employed a storekeeper.

Such names existed on our map as Avon Downs, The Ranken—here was a police outpost—Alexandria, Brunette Downs, Anthony Lagoon—another police outpost—Newcastle Waters and Daly Waters. Hereabouts we would encounter the Mataranka–Katherine–Darwin railway line and the famous Overland Telegraph Line.

Our map showed a blank white line some three inches in length for the section between Katherine and Darwin. Mileage was not shown, and the map-makers seemed not to know the distance. Nobody but a fool would ever use the track as a means of getting into Darwin. It was easier by far to wait for the weekly train.

However, we had to have our card signed in Darwin to prove we had been there with our machine, so we had no alternative other than ride that dreadful track.

We were entirely on our own now. There were no amenities at our disposal. Only the larger towns had telephones. One radio station and one only functioned in Central Australia at the time, and that was at Wave Hill station, which was not a station in the radio sense of the word at all. Rather, it was one of the largest cattle stations in the world, which was why radio communication was installed there.

Once we cleared these large cattle stations in the north and north-west of the continent we were beyond the limits of all communication with white people. The Aborigines were our only fellow beings. But since we were accompanied by a strange metal object upon which we sat and which emitted such a loud noise—and wore such strange clothing—we would have been regarded by those who saw us as creatures from another world. It was scarcely surprising that we saw precious little of our dark-skinned fellow beings.

It seemed to be by mutual agreement that we avoided each other, and we were always on our guard against attacks, which still took place. A Constable McColl was speared to death three years after our trek through the north-west!

Of course, water was of main concern. We had no idea where we could obtain it in any emergency and we had to rely solely on our two water tanks containing, when full, a total of four gallons. But 40 pounds weight in water was a severe strain on our machine and had already caused the carrier bracket to give way. The extreme roughness of the terrain often caused us to reduce our water supply unless entering on a long isolated stretch of 200 miles or so to the next human habitation.

The other main source of concern in these circumstances was fuel. Could we see the distance on our petrol-carrying capacity? We knew full well that in the event of a severe engine failure we might have to travel up to 100 miles either forward to unknown habitation or back to our previous source of supply. Then of course we had to be quite certain that our course was exact. We had no compass and steered in a general direction according to the sun. Aware that our next point for supplies would lie in one general direction, we followed the most clearly defined track leading that way. It was not always an easy thing to do. But having first established the track leaving one spot of civilisation, that was it. From then on, if uncertain of a branch track, we would even return to get fresh information on this matter. Nothing could be left to chance in these remote and inhospitable parts. Each morning we studied our previous night's camping spot and examined our position by sun-bearings, track marks, general directions, and closely investigated the spinifex grass for recent signs of breakdown by traffic, etc.

We learned all these things as we went, and only once did we take a track which led to nowhere after an eight-mile ride and have to return along the same track to our camp site to review the position in a more thorough manner. That meant sixteen miles were written off on the petrol debit side of the ledger, but as long as we stuck to a well-beaten track we felt we would not be lost.

Food would not be a problem. We carried a rifle and a

shotgun and by now we were excellent shots. Game was plentiful and we could bring down a kangaroo at 75 yards with a .22 long copper-clad cartridge with our Winchester rifle, and while in Darwin we cut down coconuts from aloft with two shots rather than climb the tree. But distance and thirst could defeat us in the wild. Would our scant water hold out for the time taken driving during the coolest time of day, to reach civilisation?

Our source of information regarding the route from one place to another was not always evident from the blueprint map we were supplied with. At times many, many miles existed between the dots on this map and from Katherine in the far north to Darwin, a total distance, according to our speedometer, of 210 miles, nothing was shown at all. We had been invited to map any such areas by the map people of Sydney, for which we would be duly paid. For those 210 miles we received £5 upon our return to Sydney.

This distance was one of the worst so-called roads one could imagine and the nearer we approached the northern coastline the more numerous were the V-shaped dry creek beds, so steep that the baseboard of the sidecar came in contact with the downward slope as the front wheel of the outfit began to climb the steep upward slope. This resulted in the baseboard becoming split for several inches, and we had to cut six inches off the board with the hacksaw to prevent the split from spreading. Our eight-gallon spare petrol tank was bolted to this section of flooring.

At times the machine could not gain the top of the opposite bank and would roll back into the trough. When this happened we had to unpack our load and repeat the attempt. One of us would then throw his weight onto the back of the machine to assist the power of the engine.

We became so tired of logging creek crossings on the map that we finally mapped only the major ones. The only other people to use these 200 miles of track were the Overland Telegraph linesmen and railway fettlers.

The wandering tribes of Aborigines were very skillful in

removing the glass insulators on the telegraph poles, so they could use them as tips on their eight-foot long spears. They reshaped the glass insulators by grinding them on a rock and fixed the resulting head to the shaft with a mixture formed from the gluey resin of the spinifex grass.

It is surprising how quickly one adjusts to suddenly observing an Aborigine striding through the trees in such extreme isolation, miles upon miles from any apparent habitation. More often than not, these tribal—or myall—Aborigines would not even acknowledge our appearance. On hearing the noise of our machine they would generally leave the common track, which was typically lined with high grass and some shrubs. We would sometimes stop to view the scene, but not a word was ever spoken. It was obviously silently agreed that we totally ignore each other under these circumstances. However, if we came upon a larger Aboriginal community we would then endeavour to form some form of communication. It was always the lubras, or womenfolk, who would step forward at our endeavour to barter tobacco for their utensils.

Then again we always kept in mind that the larger the band of Aborigines the greater was chance that a shovel-nosed spear could come whistling through the air in our direction, or a well-aimed boomerang which could easily knock a person down. After all, we carried many desirable commodities and who would ever know what had become of us? This was myall country. The Aborigines were almost the sole inhabitants of this area in 1929 and we were simply alien intruders into their domain.

We quickly learned from the scattered white population that it was better to refrain from befriending the nomads, or even making an attempt to do so; otherwise we would be regarded as 'soft' and perhaps as an easier target. I don't know how accurate these warnings were but we both decided it was prudent to heed them.

It was common practice for some Aborigines to be employed on these huge cattle stations as stockmen during the mustering season. But when the urge suddenly came upon them they would discard all the white man's clothing in their possession and go 'walkabout' and rejoin the tribe. The lubras who had domestic jobs on stations did the same. However, they retained their long, unshapely, loose-fitting outer garment commonly called a 'Mother Hubbard'.

Upon arrival at one of the little white dots marked on the blueprint map we would first seek out the Northern Territory's man of the law—the mounted trooper. Quite often there would be no-one else there anyway. At other localities there would be a general store, a small cluster of weatherbeaten houses, many roaming dogs, a few Aboriginal children, and one or two lounging Aborigines wearing huge cowboy-style hats with a colourful parrot's feather in the band, tight-fitting riding trousers, a colourful shirt and elastic-sided riding boots.

Every time, the policeman was extremely friendly and anxious to learn something of the outside world. Over the inevitable cup of tea he would outline what lay ahead of us, at least for that area within his jurisdiction. His advice regarding general conditions could always be relied upon for it was his duty to know everything that was of importance in his territory. Due to frequent meetings with his counterpart in the next district he also tended to know what could be expected there, so we gleaned important knowledge as to where we could get petrol supplies, or flour and water, and conditions of the track for the next hundred miles.

When we had covered that distance we could expect the same treatment from the next member of the Northern Territory Mounted Police.

These isolated outposts of law and order also contained a number of Aboriginal assistants, or blacktrackers, who were invaluable to the white officers. Their keen eyesight and observation of things not apparent to the white man were uncanny and their skill in following individual tracks of their own fraternity and of others with apparent ease was legendary.

Those final 200 miles into Darwin, the northern most outpost of Australia, would have been very easy to cover by simply buying a rail ticket on the once-weekly train operating between there and Katherine. It would have been simpler still to get to the western areas of the continent by bypassing Darwin altogether. This tortuous track not only took us four days of hard riding, but for each foot of the way it was always in the back of our minds that we would have to return over the same track to branch west on the next main section of our itinerary.

However, we were intent on being recognised as the first motorcycle and sidecar outfit to circumnavigate the continent, and to do this we had to present both ourselves and our outfit at the Port Darwin Post Office and have the official Auto Cycle Union of Australia's identity card stamped by the postal officials.

Artesian bores exist in a chain at fairly regular intervals where surface water is otherwise unavailable. These bores extend for a distance of some 400 miles northward to Daly Waters and became focal points in our itinerary as suitable camping spots.

No. 19 bore was located about 25 or 30 miles from Alexandria station homestead.

Northern Territory cattle stations cover up to 12,000 square miles and have several out-stations dotted here and there over this area. Our map showed No. 19 bore some distance from the homestead. Once there we could give our motor a sorely needed general overhaul.

The pump man at No. 19 was only too pleased to have somebody to talk to. He invited us to stay for a few days and to overhaul our equipment there. We agreed and he quickly produced some damper, butter and honey and made a billy of tea while we unrolled our swag and made ourselves comfortable in a corner of the huge shed which housed the pumping gear. The pump hand occupied another corner.

The next day we would commence work on our engine and try and repair the broken luggage carrier over the rear mudguard, which carried a heavy load in the two water tanks plus our swag of blankets.

Morning brought the sounds of the screeching of thousands

of galahs fighting for the first drops of water entering the long line of drinking troughs. The raucous 'caw-caw' of the crows came in as the bass tones in this symphony of sound.

A vast horde of flies was poised awaiting the first rays of the sun, which appeared within minutes—a large fiery red ball pouring its heat down upon this corner of the earth which already was dried out, cracked and parched. The flies at once commenced their attack, apparently determined not to waste any time, and we would be their target at least until the great horde of thirsty cattle arrived. Then they could take their choice.

So with this cacophony of sound we rolled from our bunks, breakfasted on damper and honey, donned our felt hats, pulled down the fly veils and prepared to commence work.

The pump hand saw to his pumping plant and made ready for the next travelling mob of cattle. Here and elsewhere, its approach would be signalled by a cloud of dust on the northern horizon. Next, a covered horse-drawn waggon would slowly approach as a vanguard to the main herd. This was the chuck waggon with the white cook and his Aboriginal offsider. Next would appear the remainder—20 or 30 horses ready for the saddle when their time came around again—then, shepherded along by the flashy Aboriginal stockmen, came the thirsty bellowing herd. Last of all was the drover.

The drover was invariably a lean, tough, sunburnt white man—typically Australian—unshaven, and covered with a fine powdery dust thrown up by the herd. He wore the usual wide-brimmed, battered felt hat and, on his feet, elastic-sided high-heeled boots. These would be surmounted by a pair of short, corrugated leggings, into the tops of which would be tucked his narrow-legged trousers.

A distance of five or six miles would separate the cook from the drover, so they met only at mealtimes and around the camp fire at night.

From time to time we were to pass through these great mobs of cattle spread widely across our track. They gave no quarter and did not yield us any right of way. While they towered above and around us with malevolent hostile looks and wide-spreading horns, we felt like pygmies as we slowly forded our may through the mob.

Somewhere amongst such a mob there must surely be one afflicted with 'pleuro'. We had been warned a pleuro bullock will charge without warning and, with this thought on our minds, we would always be mightily pleased to emerge on the far side. Here we would pause and yarn with the drover for half an hour or so.

The Aboriginal stockmen would gape at us and our strange form or transportation. They knew horses all right, better by far than we, and they had also seen a motor car or two around the homestead. But a motorcycle with a sidebox had never before entered their territory. It was as alien to them as a UFO.

However, here at No. 19 bore our UFO sadly needed attention and we lost no time in pulling the engine out of the frame to give it a major overhaul and try to prevent that infernal oil from leaking out onto each of our right boots.

It took two days to carefully overhaul the engine, renew a faulty gasket in the crankcase, decarbonise the piston heads, adjust everything, and wire up the broken water carrier with fencing wire. With this all done to our satisfaction, we shook hands with the pump man, thanked him for his hospitality and once more took to the road.

7

The Silence of the Outback

ALEXANDRIA STATION headquarters comprised a scattered assortment of wooden buildings and outhouses roofed with the inevitable corrugated iron. It was typically outback Australian. In the midst of this assortment of buildings stood the homestead with wide verandahs sheltering all four sides from the sun's fierce rays. It was usual to have one corner room wire-gauzed and otherwise open, which served as a dining room free from the otherwise ever-present flies.

Aboriginal children, stark-naked, hid at our approach, peeping around corners of the various outbuildings to view the strange-looking, noisy iron monster upon which we had arrived. Smaller children clutched their mothers' Mother Hubbards, which reached from neckline almost to the ground, and peeped at us from this scant safety. The lubras themselves stared wide-eyed at our outfit, and our strange leather breeches, high jackboots and fancy yellow high-necked sweaters with their black lettering half-hidden under our canvas riding coats.

The entire native population seemed poised for flight but took courage from the manager and his wife, who hastened forward to extend their hospitality to two 'overlanders' from the South.

We of course were delighted at the invitation to dinner and the prospect of soft beds for the night, but were a little apprehensive about our dusty clothes and general appearance. Fortunately we had taken the opportunity to clean up as much as we could while at No. 19 bore. Our shirts at least were clean, although unironed. Also in our little suitcases tucked away in the sidebox we had shoes and slacks and white shirts, so by the time we arrived at the dining table we at least presented a reasonable appearance.

It was customary on these isolated cattle stations to welcome travellers from the southern cities, invite them to stop over for the evening meal and offer them accommodation for the night. In this way these people who had no contact with the outside world except through the mail could catch up on what was going on. The mailman might come through once a week, if they were lucky.

There were two other visitors besides ourselves and it was a friendly gathering around the festive board that evening. Later we were shown our beds in the bunkhouse and on the following morning, being early risers, we arose with the station hands and at their invitation breakfasted with them.

By the time the manager's wife caught up with us to inquire as to our whereabouts for breakfast we were making ready for our departure. The good lady looked at us in surprise when we said we had breakfasted with the stockmen and remarked that she thought we had 'gone bush'. This expression was typical of these remote areas where Aborigines were employed.

We were now ready for a reasonably early start for Brunette Downs cattle station some 70 miles further along our route. Although we had not considered ourselves to be at Alexandria Station until we reached the homestead, we had actually been on the property for several days. It extended for miles in all directions and in fact No. 19 bore was on that station.

These huge cattle stations also had outstations up to some 40 or 50 miles apart, where a couple of white stockmen were stationed. Not too far distant from these outstations would be a local tribe of Aborigines together with their bark shanties, their dogs, naked children and the ever-attendant flies. The male members of the tribe would be engaged as stockmen while one or two young lubras worked in the kitchen and served at the table.

Quite a crowd had assembled to bid us farewell, and it was only then that we noticed our back tyre almost flat. In order to preserve some form of dignity we pumped it up as if this was an everyday procedure and hurriedly departed, hoping the tyre would see us to the distant horizon where we could repair it if necessary.

It was possible to see the dust from any foreign source when it was still a long way from the homestead, so we tried to get ourselves beyond the limit of dust before we stopped. This wasn't just for reasons of dignity. We did not want our kind friends taking off after us to see why we had stopped so soon after departure.

It was well past lunchtime when we finally rode into Brunette Downs homestead, and we had pumped the leaky tyre up several times in that distance.

The station cook was most apologetic that we had missed lunch. He had been advised that we were coming by Mac— one of the Brunette hands with whom we had dined the previous evening and who had returned during the night. A matter of 70 miles meant little to the locals, for this was the nearest neighbour anyway.

The cook quickly made us a meal and invited us to tuck in, all the while repeating how sorry he was that we had missed lunch.

An hour later we were on our way once more, but there was a strange sequel to this story. Two years later I pulled into a Sydney service station for petrol, and while the attendant was seeing to my needs I heard a voice I knew inside the building. I also knew the name of the owner so I went inside and there was Mac. I had dined with him at Alexandria station 2,000 miles away a couple of years earlier, and on the following day had chatted with him for a short time at Brunette Downs. It was an amazing coincidence.

The open downs country made for excellent motoring and we were able to achieve better mileage. We mistakenly felt that we could almost see Darwin, though we knew it was still a long way off, so we rode on until almost dark, hoping to camp as close as possible to Anthony Lagoon, where we knew there was a police outpost.

We didn't quite make this outpost before darkness fell and we were forced to call a halt on a gibber plain. There were so many large round stones lying about that we had to get down on hands and knees and rid the camping area of the obstructions just in order to lie down and sleep.

On occasions like this, when we stopped when we ran out of daylight, the camp was usually very austere. Generally there would be no wood, and no fire meant no food. We couldn't cook our flour and water or our turkey fillets, so we went without. To make matters worse we camped near a dead animal of some sort this night, and the smell wafted in on us on the quiet night's breeze.

Next morning we arrived at the Anthony Lagoon police outpost just in time for a cup of morning tea with the police trooper.

These men led lonely lives on their remote outposts and were more than pleased to welcome anybody who chanced by. Their job was to look after their own particular area, and sometimes they were away bush for days at a time, accompanied by one or two blacktrackers and a spare horse or two. Quite often they had to administer to the sick and injured. They also had to advise on the law, pensions, and almost anything beyond the knowledge of the local people, many of whom had had little if any schooling.

Trouble with the Aborigines was not rare and problems such as spearing cattle and tribal fights came within the jurisdiction of the local police trooper. On occasions where tribal fighting resulted in death he would bring the entire tribe into the nearest headquarters, herded together by a light chain around their necks. At nightfall he would secure them all to a tree to prevent their escape and later, aided only by his blacktrackers, bring them in for trial.

The Aborigines roamed free and far over their territory and the blacktrackers, possibly knowing the tribal area well, were of great assistance in both mounting searches and finding food and water. Tribal Aborigines were totally dependent on these sources of food and water and knew, for instance, when the waterlily roots at a certain spot would be ready for harvest, or where kangaroos could be found nearby.

However, the police trooper's life did not consist entirely of patrol work, for he also had his office chores to attend to, and in those moments he would be always prepared for a yarn with anybody from the outside world. It would be most impolite for us to pass them by.

Newcastle Waters, 182 miles away, was our longest single hop between outposts of civilisation so far. Somehow we had to try and make this goal in one day, so we did not tarry long at Anthony Lagoon. We had let the law know where we were, enjoyed the yarn and the cup of tea, and we were off.

One hundred and eighty-two miles is a long way when there is nothing, except an occasional artesian bore, over the entire distance. Not a person, black or white, not a sound, just the silence of the great Australian Outback and the noisy beat of our motor.

We sat and listened to that motor for mile after mile, instantly ready to detect the slightest defect and carefully ticking off the speedo reading right up to 91. That would be our point of no return. At such a halfway mark the rider would relay the reading to the man in the sidebox and we commenced what we termed the downhill run. Each mile brought us nearer to civilisation again. We still watched the speedo and kept an ear cocked to the sound of the motor, registering and monitoring the steady rhythmic beat.

Our blueprint map said nothing whatsoever regarding Newcastle Waters. Was it a town? Was it a lake? Was it a police outpost? Maybe it was just a name on the map. Also on the white meandering line on the blueprint appeared the one word 'Warlochs'. What the hell is—are—the Warlochs? There was nobody to tell us.

The day wore on and the distance from Newcastle Waters grew smaller and smaller. The petrol was OK and the rhythm of the motor had not faltered. The going was reasonably fair. We told each other we could walk the remaining distance now. The country had begun to change and we found ourselves on a red-coloured fine sandy loam, flat and smooth. Small leafy trees dotted the landscape and gave the area a park-like appearance. With only eighteen miles to go to Newcastle Waters we were reasonably content.

Although it was only about 4 p.m. the surroundings were enticing and, knowing we were now within reasonably easy reach of our destination, we decided to call it a day. Veering off the track, we pulled up beneath one of the shady trees, walked around to stretch our stiff limbs and gathered fallen timber for the camp fire.

The climate, too, had altered in the last hundred miles. It was quite warm and we discarded our riding coats and removed our woollen jumpers. We did not wear either of these garments again for the next 2,000 miles.

Since we had time on our hands and also had in our possession two plain turkeys and one wood duck, we decided to cook them before the warmer conditions spoiled them. We had garnered an empty petrol can along the track for this purpose. It was evidently common practice for station hands to fill their petrol tanks en route from one property to another and simply throw the empty tins away. They were ideal for our purpose. By cutting away one end of the tin, but leaving a one-inch lip to hold the fat and juices, we had a roasting pot that could hold a full turkey without dismemberment. Roast turkey! What a wonderful change from flour and water, whichever way one lives to serve it up.

We were so filled with enthusiasm we decided we would also bake a loaf of bread. Apparently we could not tear ourselves away from flour and water after all, even if we did have roast turkey for dinner and stewed duck for breakfast. When the turkey was nicely browned in the petrol-tin oven we had our dough mixed ready to take its place. Some little time later the smell of baking bread pervaded the area, rendering the surroundings even more idyllic. We were delighted, and taking our loaf from the oven decided we would bake another . . . but first let's try this one to see how good it really is.

The first incision with the knife was good enough for us.

54

Then the nicely browned and aromatic loaf disgorged a thick build-up of expanded dough which actually flowed out. We could have eaten our 'bread' with a spoon! Not that we did so. We threw the entire mess of liquid dough away.

We were loath to leave this peaceful camping spot but could not afford to tarry, and donning khaki shorts and shirts for the first time since leaving Sydney, we were on our way again the next morning.

We were now approaching what the map told us was 'Warlochs', and as we motored steadily onward we became conscious of a strange noise above that of the engine. There seemed to be an incessant hum of incoherent noises which rose in a crescendo as we narrowed the distance, until finally we came upon a chain of ponds filled to capacity with birdlife.

No wonder such a babble of noises filled the air. Each bird was vociferously demanding its right for a place in the gathering, that it might share in the delicacies offering in this chain of ponds—the Warlochs.

Here amongst all the birdlife there was not a trace of humans—nothing but hundreds upon hundreds of wildfowl of all descriptions: white ibis, pelicans, herons, and many smaller birds I couldn't identify. Stalking majestically through this gathering were jabiru storks looking for their portion of what the Warlochs had to offer. The presence of white man, and his machine, caused no disturbance to this busy scene. We were pleased to see them, and I think they might even have been pleased to see us. God knows, the country is lonely enough for birds and man to fraternise.

That is if man is not too hungry. Since we had eaten well the night before we simply silently departed with not a thought of disturbing this peaceful scene with a shotgun blast.

When we arrived at Newcastle Waters we bought a case of petrol, which cost two guineas (£2 2s 0d), and continued on our way to Katherine. That leg of the journey was not without its hazards and dangers, amongst them an unwelcome encounter with a camel.

8

Spears and Boomerangs

MAN IS SUPPOSEDLY possessed of a source of energy that is seldom tapped, except in some cases of extreme emergency. It seems to be a long-lost inheritance and is activated by what is now refered to as the subconscious mind.

I have had occasion to draw on this facility on two different occasions. Once was when an irate wild boar, challenging my right to invade his territory, charged me with a ferocity that left me bereft of conscious thought, other than to realise the hopelessness of my position. This juggernaut was within a few feet of me when a voice spoke into my inner ear—and from the inside. Quietly and softly it said, 'Step aside, one pace to the left; nice and easy'. It not only said that, but somehow it also set off the mechanism to take that step just at the right time.

The second occasion came in the Northern Territory, when I saw the camel quietly grazing on the young green shoots of the lignum break. 'That's a good snap,' I thought 'I'll take that.' Dismounting from the sidebox I set forth with the old Box Brownie Kodak and closed in on this ship of the desert for a close-up. Without any warning whatsoever the camel charged, his long neck thrust forward like the jib of a crane. As he came he opened his cavernous mouth, displaying long yellow teeth, all of which I observed in trembling fear. To add further to my fear he emitted a belligerant grunting noise which left me in no doubt as to his intentions.

In this case to simply step one pace to the left or right was entirely out of the question. This character had a long neck, flexible enough to counter any side-stepping. But once again came that softly spoken voice. 'Run,' it said. I did, and to such good effect and so fast that I surely would have lapped the camel before the first time we rounded that lignum clump!

But I had no idea what sort of a lead I had on this great smelly beast because, beyond that first grunt, there was silence—camels run on padded feet. Still, due to my lower centre of gravity I could corner far better than my adversary so I put this to great effect, rounding that break like the Road Runner!

Frank was astonished at the turn of events, but he started up the motor in great haste and rose around the lignum clump just as I appeared from the opposite direction. Without pause I vaulted into the sidebox like an Olympic hurdler and we were off.

A silent witness to the whole affair, Frank later told me that the camel was within an ace of taking a piece out of the back of my shirt. Whether he also intended to take a portion of flesh, I'll never know.

The camel episode really spurred our progress towards Daly Waters where, according to our map, there appeared to be nothing except another artesian bore. However, that meant plenty of bore water and, generally, a good supply of fallen timber for our camp fire.

Wending our way cautiously along the sandy track, we saw from time to time the footprints of dingoes. As a dingo scalp with the two ears, a strip down the back, plus the tail, would fetch us two guineas in the way of bounty, it became the duty of the sidecar passenger to supplement our meagre supply of cash in the money belt by being always at the ready with the rifle.

Mile after mile was spent in this manner, looking for unwary dingoes. Rider and passenger kept up a running commentary on their tracks.

Late one afternoon we came within sight of No. 2 bore, and as we drew nearer a dingo pup trotted out from amongst the trees. Frank quickly tensed while I slowly brought the outfit to a stop to give the chance of a sitting shot. But just as Frank was squinting along the barrel of the rifle with one eye closed I said, 'Hold it. There's somebody over there amongst those trees near the bore tank.'

Lowering the rifle, Frank and I both watched as two young lubras hurriedly departed from an Aboriginal camp for the shelter of the trees. We slowly approached, temporarily denied our good camping spot, for we had no intention of sharing the site with a group of myall Aborigines. We also felt more comfortable in the knowledge that the dingo pup still retained his scalp, both ears, the strip down the back and his tail, since it soon became obvious who owned that pup.

Upon giving the matter second thoughts, why should we leave this man-made oasis when no other suitable camping spot was available? So we decided to reconnoitre and size up the strength of the myall camp.

Taking two ducks as a peace offering we approached the mia-mia, which comprised a few branches propped against a stunted tree to form a windbreak. One or two boomerangs were lying around on the ground and three or four spears stood propped against a tree. An aged Aborigine sat crossed-legged on the ground while a middle-aged lubra clad in a Mother Hubbard advanced to meet us at what might be termed the front door. The two younger lubras were still hiding in the bush, evidently afraid of the white men or acting under orders. The dingo pup was without doubt a part of the household.

There was no sign of large numbers of myalls so we advanced, held out the two ducks and tried a few words in conversation. Neither party could understand the other but with that show of friendliness, and satisfied with the position generally, we returned to our selected spot, prepared camp and gathered wood for our fire.

Sitting around our camp fire after dark, from time to time we could hear movement in the bushes beyond the perimeter of the firelight. We knew full well the Aborigines had crept up to observe these strange white men and their still stranger machine. To these people we indeed exotic, for we were not dressed as Australian bushman generally are in cattle country in Arnhem Land. Our clothes were as unusual as our motor-bike and sidecar.

Just to make sure a spear did not come hurtling in our direction from the darkness beyond the firelight, we casually sauntered over to our sidebox and, taking the rifle from its brackets, ostentatiously squinted down the barrel and ejected cartridges in quick succession, aiming at some imaginary target together with a mild searchlight display with the Winchester flashlight. The noises outside our field of vision ceased.

Daybreak revealed the same group of Aborigines—namely, one aged buck, one aged lubra, and two young gins. As a parting show of friendliness and goodwill I walked across and made a present of a further brace of ducks we had shot for the larder during the previous day's run, then returned to our campsite, jumped on the kick-starter, revved up the motor and sped off in a cloud of dust. Fortunately our dusky neighbours at No. 2 bore had not known how close their mongrel dog had come to being two guineas' worth of ears and tail.

We were now on our way to Katherine, a small town at the southern extremity of the north–south railway from the port of Darwin. This meant we were well into Arnhem Land; a huge area of Northern Australia teeming with all kinds of wildfowl, thanks to the numerous rivers and their tributaries which flattened out here and there forming swamps, marshes and lagoons. The region was also host to wild buffalo and crocodiles.

The entire area was a reserve for the wandering Aborigines, although a few whites had set up camps along the rivers where they hunted buffalo for the hides which were transported to Darwin by water. From now on we could expect to meet up with nomad Aborigines at any time from here right across to the distant border of Western Australia.

Almost daily we would see footprints made by bare feet in the sandy track right under our front wheel.

One one occasion we followed footprints in the sand for ten miles, picking them up again the following morning, but we never did see the person who seemed to us to be on a marathon walkabout. Strangely, it never dawned on us that the makers of these footprints could be standing quietly hidden behind a tree watching us pass by.

Occasionally we came upon a lone native carrying a bundle of long glass-tipped spears over his shoulder but it was standard practice for white men to pass on without so much as a nod of the head. This, we were told, was the done thing. It was then the common theory amongst the drovers and stockmen that an Aborigine must be kept in his place. To this end a notice was displayed on a verandah post outside a small Chinese store in the little township of Pine Creek—'Dogs and Aboriginals registered here'.

The tribal Aborigines' survival depended upon their skill and efficiency with spear or boomerang. When it came to larger game such as the kangaroo, the spear became the prime weapon. The boomerang was used mainly for hunting the larger species of ground birds such as the plain turkey or bustard. A throwing stick was also used for smaller game.

The spear being the prime weapon, it was made with great care. With the arrival of the white man came the glass bottle, and then the glass insulators on the Overland Telegraph wires. Once the natives had learned the value of glass as a cutting implement they quickly realised how they could modernise spear points by fashioning them in this material. To obtain the glass it was a simple matter to climb the slender wrought-iron pole of the telegraph line, cut the wire, remove the insulator and then disappear into the hinterland. And so, as we progressed upon our way, we were asked to keep an eye open to see where the wire was down . . . and would we kindly reattach same to restore communication with the south?

The racing motorist of modern times, hell-bent on record-breaking, would rarely be called upon to effect repairs on broken telegraph lines. Then again, he would not be expected to wonder where his next meal was coming from, or if the next cattle station manager would be good enough to sell him a case of petrol, and could he also spare a pound or two of flour and a bit of sun-dried meat from atop the wood pile.

At any rate, the Aborigine of northern Australia slowly started on the long road to the white man's way of life—by becoming the proud possessor of a glass-tipped spear. Frank and I also became the proud possessors of several of these spears, thanks to our barter system—four sticks of white man's tobacco for one spear. These prides of our possession were somewhat longer than the sidebox and the overhang sadly proved their undoing. Within the first two days we had broken our glass points from their anchorage by taking short cuts around our sidebox instead of making a more circuitous route from front to rear. However, our boomerangs, also procured under the barter system, remained intact for the full distance and still adorn the walls of my home. Of course we still procured our game with the rifle or shotgun and never at any time tried to emulate the native by dropping our bird with a boomerang throw. Instructions on how to get your bird did not come with the boomerang. Nor did we issue instructions as to the use of white man's tobacco, and whether they chewed it or smoked it I shall never know.

The area north of Katherine was completely unmapped for motorists, not that many motor vehicles or their drivers braved this area. We did, however, occasionally come across an entomologist in an old car who was conducting research on the buffalo fly.

Spear grass seven feet high lined the track on both sides and the man in the saddle was kept perpetually busy, first with the left gauntletted hand kept raised before his face to prevent injury from the overhanging grass, and next the right hand had to quickly release the right-hand twist grip which was the throttle control to avoid knuckle damage from sapling trees hitting the handlebar. In his spare time it was necessary to steady the violent up and down motion of the sidebox to reduce damage to its springs and chassis. There wasn't much time for any other duties except to pull the heavy machine around the sandy lumpy bends in that tortuous track—and the grass, trees, and sand all fought back.

61

This track had been formed by four-wheeled vehicles of standard width. But since our outfit was narrower, the sidecar wheel rode high on the space between the wheel tracks. Not only did this throw us over on an angle which added considerably to the strain of negotiating bends, but it took its toll on the knuckles of driver's right hand as he slewed towards the young trees growing alongside the track. From time to time the track just fizzled out so we followed a course between the trees wherever we could comfortably pass, veering left or right in accordance with where the Overland Telegraph Line lay. We could not go wrong provided we always remembered upon which side the OT line should be.

At Katherine we immediately called into the police station for the usual cup of tea and a yarn with the trooper and his wife. Katherine was quite a town compared with the other police outposts along the track. Here we were advised to offload all the surplus gear and to travel as lightly as possible over the rugged, rarely used track into Darwin.

The map gave no details whatever regarding conditions between Katherine and Darwin, or even the distance, so we decided to record mileages and outstanding features considered to be of some use in mapping this section.

From here on the track all but lost its identity, but we remained aware of where we were in relation to the railway line and the OT. We had to keep both in mind whenever a left-right-hand fork appeared, as many of these led away into lonely buffalo camps well off our course.

At one such fork we were astonished to see a well-dressed white girl mounted on a beautiful horse—just as if she had stepped out of a Hollywood location shot. She just sat there like a statue and looked. We were so surprised and self-conscious we didn't even stop. Whether she had prior knowledge of our approach and had ridden into the main track from her family's camp I do not know, though we learned later on in Darwin that she was the daughter of a well-known buffalo hunter.

It was astonishing how the Aborigines at buffalo camps

could tell that we were due at a certain place, more or less at a certain time, but it happened. Suddenly a worker would say to his white overseer, 'Im close-up now, boss. White fella come.'

There was always a group of Aborigines around the buffalo camps, where they helped in the hunt and the skinning of the buffalo in return for niki-niki—blackfellows' tobacco—and tucker.

In the meantime, however, we had to get to Darwin to have our card stamped. So we battled along those miles of unused track which only became worse and worse. The closer we came to the coast, the more we were confronted with narrow streams, creek gullies and heavily timbered country. Creek crossings became so frequent we only recorded those that we considered as a landmark for future motorists. But for us each crossing was hazardous, whether we mapped it or not. The sidecar suffered most, but we generally managed to get through without off-loading all our gear.

At the end of a day's ride between Katherine and Darwin the average mileage was only 50. And for four whole days, from daylight until dark, we reminded each other that we would be coming back over this again in a few days.

What a trip! We were averaging six miles an hour over this terrible stretch of non-road, and this was our way of taking a holiday. By nightfall we were exhausted but undaunted, and after a frugal breakfast we set off once again for some more of this slow torture.

Finally we came to the Adelaide River. Here was a noble stream compared to our vicious creek crossings, and here also was a large tribe of Aborigines. Shovel-nosed spears stood propped against trees, and boomerangs lay upon the ground.

The natives were naked except for the traditional naga—a small piece of bark or dirty cloth hanging suspended from a string around the waist. Rear view was only the string. Their chests were ribbed like scrubbing boards, the corrugations being formed by cutting open the flesh at regular intervals and filling the open cut with ash, leaving a ridging effect on the chest.

Quickly sizing up their numerical strength, we decided that a camp alongside the gently flowing Adelaide River was not for us, and hitting the water of the crossing with as much speed as was needed to gain the opposite bank, we left the astonished natives to wonder amongst themselves as to what the white man was going to do next. Maybe we didn't mind dying of thirst on the Madmans Track later on, or lying alongside it with a broken leg until some chance overlander or telegraph linesman ultimately found our skeletons, but we certainly decided against the possibility of death by a shovel-nosed spear.

It was a pity to lose the luxury of flowing water at the Adelaide and the more so when we examined the camp site we had been forced to choose. However, it was too dark to ride any further so we made the best of things in the usual manner.

Our fire was unusually small that night as we cooked our johnnycakes and boiled the billy. The mosquitoes having joined us, we rigged up our mosquite net, crawled underneath it and composed ourselves to sleep. Before long a long drawn-out note of a curlew broke the silence of the darkness, shortly followed by another and yet another until it seemed we were surrounded by them. It became obvious to us that the Aborigines had found us, for curlews do not call to each other in such numbers, and from so many points of the compass.

We had overlooked the fact that our engine made such an unholy noise in this part of the world that we were reasonably easy to locate. So we crawled from beneath the mosquite net, took out our rifle, the Browning automatic pistol and the Winchester torch, and sallied forth amongst the trees, flashing the torch beams from left to right. The curlew noises stopped immediately and we returned to the mosquito net, crawled under it once more and fell asleep.

At first light, and without any breakfast, were on our way. The natives were probably just inquisitive and had probably never before seen a three-wheeled contraption such as ours. Nevertheless, spearings were still the fashion in these parts and our caution was reasonable enough.

After four days on this terrible apology for a track we finally came out of timbered country and found ourselves at 'the two and a half mile' which denoted the edge of the town of Darwin. In fact it was fairly obvious to us that we couldn't be too far from the coast because we could smell salt in the air. It was one month exactly since we had left Sydney.

9

A Bright Idea

PORT DARWIN was separated from the rest of Australia by thousands of trackless miles. At the time of our arrival there were only three ways of getting there. One was overland—that was our method. The others were by the railway we were sadly prevented from using, or by the monthly boat from Sydney which journeyed up the east coast, through the Torres Strait, touching at Thursday Island, then entered the Arafura Sea and made for Cape Don. The voyage took about one month.

The only way freight could come in was by sea in this slow and tedious fashion. Therefore all the shops' merchandise became expensive to buy and, unless locally produced, could become in short supply. Clothing was made up by Chinese tailors who sat in front of their shops with their foot-pedalled sewing machines on the dirt footpath making white drill suits for the few white men fortunate enough to be able to afford them.

Cavanagh Street was the main thoroughfare. It boasted a straggly row of wooden shanties whose verandahs, supported by round timber poles, overhung the footpath. A motley collection of town Aborigines lounged idly in the shade provided by the verandahs. All the roofs were covered with galvanised corrugated iron. Most of these shops were owned and operated by Chinese.

No white women were to be seen along Cavanagh Street, except one. After enquiring where we had come from, and why, she began to extol the virtues of the British race, made some references to the 'Bulldog Breed' and called upon the nearby Chinese and natives for three hearty cheers, adding at the termination of this exercise, 'We still have them.'

Her cryptic words no doubt referred to the 'Bulldog Breed'. We just stood there in silence and wondered why we should have been more or less introduced in such a strange and impromptu manner to a still stranger collection of humanity.

We had in our possession a letter of introduction to a Mr Jack Cooper of Darwin. Upon reading this letter from his sister in Sydney, he welcomed us with the utmost hospitality and initiated us into a bachelor style of accommodation amongst several of his friends. We stayed here the four days we were in Darwin, during which time Jack took time off work to escort us and show the sights. Prominent amongst these were the botanical gardens and Fanny Bay Gaol.

Fanny Bay Gaol was a primitive temporary structure walled by high galvanised corrugated iron sheeting. I doubt that there was another gaol like it anywhere in Australia.

One day a prisoner went missing, but just as darkness was falling there came a loud hammering on the gaol gates. It was the missing prisoner clamouring to be let in. He angrily demanded to know why he had been locked out and complained that he had almost missed the evening meal. 'Escape?' he asked his accusers. Where in hell do you think I'd escape to? Walk over two hundred miles to Katherine to be picked up and brought back?'

When one considers Darwin's isolation at that time, it seemed a fair question. There was nowhere one could escape to and the prisoner had only been asleep down along Mendel beach.

Those four days in Darwin were a welcome holiday for us. The hospitality shown by our new bachelor friends, living in a kind of male commune, saved us from hotel expenses and we only had to buy one meal a day at a Chinese cafe at low cost. But even this was a drain on what was left of our £60, and we still had two-thirds of our journey to complete.

We whiled away those four days with Jack Cooper, wandered along Mendel beach and inspected the burial ground of the Melville Island natives with its strange-looking carved totem poles. We shot down coconuts with our .22 rifle and drank the sweet milk, and we even went to the Saturday night cinema.

It was an open-air affair with whites seated in deckchairs down the front and blacks and 'other ranks', including us, on hard seats up the back of the enclosure. A minor fracas broke out not far from us at one stage. Apparently somebody hit 'Brother Francis' over the head with a bag of oranges. At interval everybody adjourned to the neighbouring vacant allotment and attended to the call of nature en masse, some squatting and some standing, all in accordance with their sex.

We also took time off to make a minor overhaul of our equipment, but everything seemed to be in reasonable order.

After four days we simply could not afford to stay any longer. A distant relative of mine who had a buffalo camp away over in Arnhem Land invited us to stay there and enjoy ourselves. But it would be several weeks before he was due to return, so that was not possible either.

The day dawned when we said goodbye to all those men who had befriended us and started back once more on that tough 200-mile track to Katherine, where we were to pick up the belongings we had left at the police station and then head west for Wave Hill, Wyndham, and Derby. This was regarded as the 'second leg' of our journey, and by far the most adventurous and forbidding. It was even said that the natives of the Kimberleys were hostile to all white men.

When we arrived back at the two and a half mile on the edge of town we had a bright idea. Why not ride along the railway line over the sleepers? It couldn't possibly be as bad as that track with all those creeks and gullies which had almost wrecked the sidebox. There was only one train a week into Darwin and it was not due that day. We didn't give a thought to the possibility of any other rail traffic. All we had fixed in our minds was how to avoid that bush track. So we took to the rail track.

The machine fitted nicely between the rails and the going was just great. What a surprise any engine driver would get had he suddenly been confronted with two characters driving up to meet him on a Harley-Davidson motorcycle with sidecar attached. However, we found we had erred badly before anything so extraordinary could occur. Riding happily along between the rails we once more came upon one of our cursed creek crossings. The railway engineers had seen fit to bridge the creek with a high embankment, but the rails strung across the intervening gap were on sleepers spaced so far apart that the front wheel of our machine would surely have fallen through had we not stopped in time.

Here we were, then, high up on a railway embankment from which there was no escape other than by lifting the heavy outfit over the rails and, with all wheels locked sliding down to the bottom. Then we would have to relocate the track we so fondly thought we had avoided.

And this is what we did. We fought our way back to the Adelaide River. The myalls had gone but the mosquitoes were still there, so once again we deemed it wise to camp elsewhere. The going seemed marginally better on the return trip and we arrived back at Katherine in almost one day less than on the outward journey.

We collected our spare luggage, told the police trooper of our adventures covering those rugged 420 miles and packed up once more. Our thoughts were now fixed on a westerly direction rather than the northerly one we had been on for the past month.

10

'The Madman's Track'

As WE RODE the track to Wyndham and Derby, we both were fully aware of the problems that could confront us. For a start, there were next to no means of communication available. If we struck trouble anywhere on this leg we would have to get ourselves out of it. We also knew we had many rivers to cross and we would have to decide how we would do this when we got there. Amongst these rivers was the bugbear of them all, the dreaded Fitzroy. We had heard much of the Fitzroy Crossing. It was famous. Now it lay before us as a giant challenge.

Few people had ever been across this track. Some who had started out had not been heard of again, so information was scant and quite often such as there was was not correct. Somewhere out there was what was known as the 'Madman's Track', but just where we did not know. We did know, however, that at Wave Hill—a huge cattle station about halfway to Wyndham—there was a powerful radio transmitter capable of relaying messages to the southern cities. This radio had recently been brought into prominence during the search for the lost aeroplane the *Southern Cross* when Kingsford Smith and his co-pilot Charles Ulm were reported overdue at Wyndham. Apart from this remote link with the rest of Australia, nobody would hear of us until we arrived at Wyndham, Halls Creek, Derby or Broome. It was to be three or four weeks before we could once more be accounted for. During that period we could hit a tree, wreck our outfit, break a leg or die of thirst. No one would know.

Similar risks had applied over the trip into Darwin, but on that section of the journey we were never far from the Overland

70

Telegraph Line. In case of dire necessity we had only to cut this low-slung wire and wait. Within a day or two a linesman would arrive seeking the fault in the line.

On our present course there were distances of up to 400 miles to be covered between supplies of petrol, and hundreds of long lonely miles between one cattle station and its neighbour. We therefore put our trust in providence and upon our skill to keep the engine going every day and all day. Without that engine's musical note we would need bushcraft skills we didn't have if we were to survive.

We travelled 80 atrocious miles westward from Katherine, mostly over heavy sandy tracks where our engine laboured to keep us steadily on our way, then through a long rough patch of black soil evidently trampled by wild buffalo and hardened by the sun. The rider was up and down on the saddle like a yo-yo for sixteen miles while the engine did its best in low gear. What a drain on the petrol supply this was.

Towards evening the motor came to a halt of its own accord. Here indeed was trouble and we quickly reviewed our position. Forty miles onwards lay Willeroo Station; 80 miles behind us was Katherine. There was no assistance closer at hand. Our provisions consisted of three or four pounds of plain flour, a tin of treacle and a couple of gallons of water.

We had, of course, our shotgun and rifle, and we were well stocked with ammunition. As the day was almost spent, and having established that things were not too good generally, we promptly set fire to our surroundings within a reasonable distance around us to rid us of any vermin which might be lurking nearby, spread out our blankets on that burnt ground and decided to sleep on the problem. We had some replacement parts with us, but were they the ones we needed? Tomorrow we would know one way or the other.

If the worst came to the worst we would abandon the outfit and commence walking the 80 miles back to Katherine, carrying the two gallons of water with us, and our flour. At Katherine we could telegraph the Harley-Davidson agency for whatever spares we required. They could then despatch the article by the monthly boat from Sydney to Darwin, from where it could be forwarded to Katherine by the once-weekly train. Then all we had to do was walk the 80 miles back to our abandoned vehicle and commence work. All this could take two, to three months.

By the time we retired for the night we had determined that the engine failure was most likely caused by the magneto. We had no spare parts for magneto repairs, so things looked grim.

We were eagerly astir at dawn. There was no wood handy for a fire so we ate remnants of a loaf of bread purchased in Katherine, and commenced work. We pulled the maggie to pieces, carefully examined each part, cleaned everything and put it together again. By this time the sun was well past the meridian. Well, this was it. Would the motor start, or was this the end of the venture?

We jumped on the kick-starter and the motor roared into life. It was music to our ears, beautiful music. The magneto has simply oiled up. Jubilant at hearing the roar of the motor once more, we lost little time in vacating that unsavoury spot.

Towards the middle of the afternoon we arrived at Willeroo homestead, where we were surprised to be greeted by a white woman. There were practically no white women at all in this part of Australia at that time, and the very few who left the cities behind were usually to be found only in the sparsely settled townships dotted here and there along the track. This woman was the wife of the station manager who was away mustering cattle on some distant part of the property.

When she learnt of our breakdown and heard that we had not eaten for almost two days she promptly organised the native women in the kitchen and prepared a meal for us. She was excited at having new people to talk to, but from time to time she would lapse into pidgin out of habit. She spoke nothing else in the household for days on end while her husband was absent at remote parts of the station.

Besides giving us a good meal, our kind hostess insisted on our accepting bread and meat to take along with us. We thanked her for the meat and the hospitality and, hoping to make Delamere station before darkness, sped off.

In this lonely, dry country only Aborigines seemed to know where to find underground water in what are known as soaks. Scratch a few inches under the soil and if one was in the right place there would be a minimal amount of good drinking water. However, the local tribes were said to keep the soaks cunningly concealed. It was therefore necessary for us to carry enough water to get us to where we wanted to go.

The low hills surrounding Delamere homestead gave me a peculiar eerie feeling. I felt as if I were being watched from some of the surrounding hilltops and quite likely I was not far wrong, for as we rode into the homestead yard I could hear dogs yapping, the laughter of natives and the play of children from an Aboriginal camp just beyond a small knoll.

We were ushered into the unpretentious homestead by the head stockman, who introduced us as two overlanders to his two assistants, who were the sole white occupants of this out-station. Two or three young lubras were busily engaged in the kitchen helping the white cook prepare the evening meal amongst much giggling and laughter. The meals generally consisted of corned beef, potatoes and damper.

Three native women served the evening meal in a shy and frightened manner. They seemed ready to take flight at any moment as, although they were quite accustomed to the stock-men, we were an unknown quantity, and there was that iron monster upon which we had arrived still standing at the back door.

The meal finished, the head stockman took up the running. He evidently fancied himself as a man who could tell a good story and entered into a lengthy narration of how he had to chastise an Aborigine once, which led to a bout of fisticuffs. He remembered every blow taken and given, for as he said: 'This young "boong" was bloody good. I feinted with the left and hooked him with a right cross but the young bugger connected with his right to my head. He was bloody good all right. Anyway . . . ' and here he would rise and slowly walk across and take a drink of water from one of the water cans.

73

'Now as I was saying . . . ' Here a younger stockman, being an excitable man, could not restrain his pent-up excitement would say, in a foreign accent, 'Yes, but how did you finish up?' 'Wait on,' replied the head stockman, 'I'm coming to that,' and knowing full well how agitated his assistant was he would deliberately pause to light his pipe, let the match die out, say 'bugger it', strike another match and slowly light his pipe, all the while summing up the general position to see how he was going.

Meanwhile the cook, who had probably heard this tale often—had taken himself off to the kitchen. Judging by the playful screams and laughter of the gins he was evidently up to some trick. When the storyteller had the young stockman fairly dancing with excitement and wanting once more to know 'Yes, but how you finish up?' he finished that tale and went on to a sequel. In that story he told how, on the following day, he walked into the corral to select a horse for the day's work, but having got amidst the milling horses could not remember what he was in there for, so walked out again to figure it out. Finally his brain cleared and all was well.

It was not often that the head stockman had such an appreciative audience and he took full measure of time to give a blow-by-blow account of all his high jinks.

Next morning Frank and I sat on our accustomed seats, he on the flour tin, I on the meat tin, under a stunted tree and ate our damper and treacle. Two insignificant figures in this huge expanse of wasteland. As we ate we gazed mutely out upon the glaring, sun-bleached, parched surroundings, sparsely covered with dry thorn and stunted trees which appeared more dead than alive. We both knew that within four miles of where we now sat in this lonely forbidding spot in the Tanami Desert, two famous Australian airmen, Hitchcock and Anderson, had perished when their plane, the *Kookaburra*, had made a forced landing.

The *Kookaburra* had made a hasty departure from Sydney in the search for Charles Kingsford Smith and Charles Ulm when they were reported overdue somewhere in the north of

Australia. The *Kookaburra* was forced to land when it developed engine trouble. The pilot and navigator fixed the minor fault but found there was not enough space available to become airborne again. They pushed over as many of the dead trees as they could to lengthen their primitive runway but at the end of their efforts the plane was still grounded. Their two bodies were later found under the wings of the plane, where they had crawled to escape the blistering sun.

Wave Hill station, which had been the centre of search operations for the two missing planes, was our next petrol supply base. Since the petrol was brought in for the search operations by camel team we had to pay more than four times city prices for this precious fluid. Had the ill-fated crew of the *Kookaburra* only known, they were within walking distance of Wave Hill.

After silent contemplation of the surroundings, Frank and I realised it would be a hell of a place to be lost without food or water. A matter of two or three days would see the end. We picked up our respective tins and packed up. Thankful when our motor roared into life again, we left the dismal scene. An hour later we rode into Wave Hill homestead yard.

We were always well received at these huge cattle stations. Our arrival almost always seemed to coincide with either lunch or dinner time, and we were always invited to share this meal. In fact refusal on our part would have appeared most unsociable.

News of the outside world was scarce enough as it was and a meal was an excellent opportunity to hear from travellers; or 'overlanders' as we were called. It was rare indeed when we moved on from a homestead towards the close of day, rather than stay for dinner and bed down for the night. However, since we had dined under our scanty shade only seven or eight miles back, it was still too early to call it a day and filling our tanks with the precious and costly fuel—enough for the next 400 miles—we made ready for the next burst. Best to get the ghosts of those airmen behind us.

To carry petrol for 400 miles to our next known source of

supply we bought one and one half cases. That is three four-gallon tins. After filling all our tanks we still had several gallons which had to be stored somewhere, so the spare tin was lodged between the knees of the passenger in the sidebox. We didn't always have the utmost of comfort in this jaunt of ours. However, by now we seemed to be travelling in convoy as two other men were going in our direction by Chevrolet car. One of these was the entomologist who was researching the buffalo fly. We had previous linked up with our fellow travellers over on the Darwin side of the continent.

Our next haven was to be Inverway. A relatively small property compared to Wave Hill and Victoria River Downs, Inverway was owned and run by the three Farquharson brothers who had spent the greater part of their lives in this territory. Well past middle-age, they still drove their own herds of marketable cattle into Wyndham meatworks. We had been warned that there was not a motorised piece of equipment on the place, so we had to carry extra fuel with us.

Some distance out from Wave Hill the back tyre cut on a stone and deflated with a loud report. There was no doubt about that, we had a flat. Upon investigation, we removed the tyre and threw it away—just like that. It was beyond repair. This meant we now had only one spare. We had been telling each other for days now that the back tyre would see us round to Perth, but we were wrong.

A mile or so further on the carrier for our water tanks broke. Each tank weighed over 40 pounds when full and this, plus the weight of our swag, was eventually too much for the carrier. All our attempts at repairing it were in vain.

We struggled along with this piece of faulty equipment until at last we had to make camp for the night. The only spot available seemed to be in the middle of a vast plain. There was no reason to expect to suddenly come upon a green oasis in this forbidding area and, as always, darkness forced us to discontinue our efforts for the day.

It seems a strange way of living to simply stop in the middle of an arid desert, lie down on the bare dusty ground and sleep.

Not even a wild animal would do that; it would at least have some favoured sleeping spot. This was not for us, however, and tired, foodless and unable even to light a fire, we spread our blankets and decided the only thing to do was sleep.

It was then that a bull, apparently keen to investigate this blot upon his territorial demesne, bore down on our sparse camp in belligerent fashion and with much loud bellowing.

Under these conditions it had always been my boyhood procedure to scale the nearest available fence and keep going at a reasonably high speed. Alternatively I could hide behind a large tree and slowly circle, or quickly circle, as circumstances demanded. But here the nearest fence was miles away, and there was not a tree to be seen this side of the horizon. All we could do was to cower in close to our trusty machine, which to the irate animal must have looked like nothing else other than a heap of scrap iron. We could perhaps have challenged his bellowing by mounting the machine and starting up the motor, which at this stage of our journey could possibly have out-bellowed any animal.

However, our antagonist apparently realised that this heap of old junk in no way diminished his grazing rights or challenged his manhood, so he wandered off into the night, leaving us in complete possession. This was only the second time our camp had been disrupted by animals of the night.

The next morning we continued to wrestle with the troublesome carrier. We must have our water; no-one can afford to throw that away. By this time we had at least managed to drain our surplus petrol into the tank, thus relieving the passenger of a four-gallon tin between his hunched-up knees. During one of the many attempts to secure the carrier our friends with the Chev arrived in a cloud of dust, also bound for Inverway. There was not much they could do, however, so they sped on.

The day was dwindling fast and the sun was low in the sky when a cloud of dust appeared behind us, indicating yet another traveller. Quickly the cloud of dust approached and, lo and behold, here once more were our friends in the Chev.

They had taken another track since parting with us and after many miles found themselves at a dead end. Fortunately for us we had not followed their tracks. Such a mistake could have left us with an empty petrol tank, although we were to make the same error ourselves later on.

As our dusty friends were within petrol range of Wyndham, they sped on once more, with the assurance that if we were not in at Inverway that night they would come and look for us in the morning. We felt like lame ducks as we watched their dust fade so quickly.

Then came our brainwave. We disconnected the broken carrier, complete with water tanks and swag, and gave them the sole use of the sidebox. The passenger took up a pillion position at the rear upturned section of the bucket saddle while the rider slid forward on the same saddle. We were off like the wind and arrived at Inverway together with the Chev, both in the same cloud of dust.

The Farquharson brothers must have thought it was an invasion and we certainly presented a less than wonderful picture. These cattle men really must have thought what lunatics we were to be riding around Australia, both on the one saddle. But in this case we had to take our hats off to the horseman who the next morning showed us how to make a Cobb & Co hitch. He repaired our carrier in about ten minutes with a piece of fencing wire and brought this rattling, troublesome piece of equipment completely under control. The carrier lasted all the way back to Sydney without further trouble.

That same morning our friends of the road left us and took off for Wyndham. We had no reason for going there and figured we would have enough petrol to take us to Nicholson station on the Western Australian border. We were taking a chance here, for nobody could tell us where petrol could be obtained except at Wyndham and Halls Creek—a small town in the Kimberleys which lay directly in our path, although just beyond the limits of our petrol supply. But we didn't fancy a 90-mile ride just to buy petrol, so it was a case of Halls Creek or walk!

My diary shows that the average daily run in these areas and for the past few days was between 89 and 109 miles at an average speed of 8 to 13 mph. In fact these mileages are typical of each day's efforts for the next 2,000 miles, and we could not do better until we were within a few miles of Perth. This does not necessarily mean that the entire day was spent doing 12 mph. Quite often we could roar along at 40 mph or even better, but sometimes it would take an hour or more to negotiate just one dry river crossing. And in spinifex country, where the sidecar wheel rode over the tufty spinifex clumps, we had to restrict the speed to prevent the outfit rattling to pieces.

Since the track was almost indiscernable and signposts, of course, were nonexistent, we decided which of two divergent tracks we would take by maintaining a general sense of direction and keeping one eye on the sun in relation to the approximate time of day.

On the only occasion we took a wrong track we knew full well that it was not heading where it should have been. But since this misleading track was far more well worn and spinifex grass all but hid the one we should have taken, we expected the track we took to swing south-west at any time.

In driving towards Nicholson station we were also getting into the river country around the north-west coastline, where we knew there were five or six rivers to cross. Most forbidding of all was the Fitzroy Crossing. We hoped to be there in a day or two.

The country was dead flat and quite uninteresting, without even an Aboriginal camp or kangaroo to be seen. This would be one of the driest areas in the north.

Arriving at Nicholson around midday we enquired about petrol supplies but our luck was out. We next enquired about kerosene, as we could start the motor on petrol and switch our spare tank onto kero. Here again we met with failure. There was no quantity available to serve our purpose. At lunch with the manager of the property in a huge wired-in room like a birdcage, we were told that a woodcutter was employed at a camp about 25 miles further on, and that he used a utility truck to cart the wood into Halls Creek.

We used every device known to motoring to cut down our petrol consumption. On every slight decline we would switch the motor off and coast, even for a few hundred yards. We would cut the motor and roll to a stop whenever we decided to pull up, but we still fell short of the woodcutter's camp by four miles, so we got out and pushed. Luckily the country was almost flat and we arrived after about one and a half hours. The woodcutter let us have two gallons of petrol which we knew would get us into Halls Creek.

We stayed at the camp that night and felt quite relieved to know that at long last petrol supplies were once again attainable. We had travelled well over 400 miles since our last supply, and from now on were within range of West Australian coastal towns as we turned south and headed for Broome.

But the worst was yet to come. We still had to fight our way through the Kimberleys and cross the Margaret, Laura and Fitzroy Rivers. And we still had 50 miles to go before we reached Hall's Creek, our first Western Australian town.

From a distance the Kimberley Range appeared to be a series of low hills covered with spinifex and no other vegetation. When we entered the foothills we found our track to be rough and rock strewn. Our mileage dropped to little more than a walk in this rough going. After negotiating a small creek we came upon a small party of tribal Aborigines and we pulled up, partly out of curiosity and partly thinking we might trade some nicki-nicki (cheap tobacco) that we had purchased in Darwin for boomerangs, spears or throwing sticks. It was not considered altogether safe to turn one's back on the true myall, so we carefully arranged to set the scene for barter. Frank leant casually with his rump against the outfit, facing the natives at all times and with the automatic Browning in his coat pocket, while I approached, holding the nicki-nicki for all to see and reciting what I had rehearsed for mile upon mile. 'White man gibbet nicki-nicki, black man gibbet spear.'

A fine athletic warrior sat down as I approached and refused to enter into any discussion. However, I saw the glint in the eyes of the lubras, who quickly interpreted my proposal. No dice. He would not budge. So I marched back to the outfit while Frank covered my every move and we got started again. Upon rounding a bend we again halted, whereupon two of the lubras approached us from a low gully and said 'Gibbet boomerangs'. I said 'Gibbet nicki-nicki or shillun'. They said 'Nicki-nicki and shillun'. I laughed and said 'Oh no' and handed over the four sticks of tobacco in exchange for four war boomerangs. We lined the two lubras up and took their photo, which left them giggling and apparently well pleased with the deal—but with no shilling.

We still had sixteen miles of atrocious road to cover before we arrived at Halls Creek. In accordance with our usual practice, the first port of call was the police station.

The policeman's wife immediately invited us in for a cup of tea and during this interlude the constable advised us that it may be a good idea if we avoided the vehicle registration authority in the small township in case he asked us to pay a road tax upon our entry into the state.

Some months after our return to Sydney an article appeared in a Sydney newspaper with the headline ' "Pay Up," said the Bobby, "or leave".' Then followed the story of how 'the Bobby' had ordered us to either pay up or get out of town. All I can hope is that the good constable and his wife never read that untrue story.

11

River Crossings

AFTER LEAVING the little mining township of Halls Creek we negotiated rough sandy tracks and spinifex for mile after mile. The sidecar wheel bounced from clump to clump over the spinifex grass. If only we could have extended that wheel another twelve inches, so our wheels were a car's width apart, it would have been a much smoother ride for the passenger, and for both of our nervous systems. That continuous pounding was certainly not going to favour the already worrying springing of the sidecar chassis, and upon a minute inspection, sure enough, the casting was already showing a small fracture.

On that bumpy ride from Halls Creek and Derby we were also committed to go twelve miles out of our way to deliver the mail to Moora-Boola Aboriginal station. It was common practice to at times carry the few letters or telegrams from one small township to an outlying property rather allow a wait of perhaps several weeks between the regular mailman's trips. We therefore decided that since we had to go out of our way into the Aboriginal station we would, when we arrived, see what we could do about the fractured sidecar chassis to prevent it from becoming worse.

First, however, we had to cross the Margaret River, which lay between Halls Creek and Fitzroy. To cross these northern rivers one had to simply ignore the passage of time. It might take us from one to two hours of laborious work before we gained the opposite bank, but having arrived at the Margaret, and in accordance with our usual procedure, we dismounted and walked up and down along the steep bank to determine the best point of entry at which to make our crossing. Then we girded up our loins and using low gear and full throttle pelted down the steep bank in somewhat reckless fashion to hit the water at full speed, hoping the motor would get us beyond the water before phasing out. Beyond that water lay an expanse of heavy sand right across to the opposite bank.

Our impetus down the steep bank carried us through the water, but then the real work began. The passenger took up a position behind the sidebox and pushed while the rider kicked madly with his free foot at the sandy surface to gain every pound of assistance. The other foot was of course on the clutch pedal, for immediate use if necessary. No, we couldn't make it under these conditions so we held a council of war—man against the river. We allowed the motor to cool down and once more took up our stations. Finally, we reached the opposite bank ... but was it? To our dismay we had only arrived on a small island, and beyond this lay more of the Margaret River, every bit as wide as the part we had laboriously negotiated. We were disappointed, but we were exhausted and could go no further, so we decided to eat, and then rest. While resting we cogitated on ways and means of crossing sandy river beds, now and in the future. We had several more known rivers to cross.

Any other species than man would have tackled our problem by sheer strength, and lacking that strength would have given up and gone around it, if that were possible. However, since we lacked the strength and could not go around, we had to go across. So having eaten our flour and treacle, and rested, and cogitated, we now arose to conquer the next passage of the Margaret River. With the motor now cooled down we drove into the heavy sand until the exhausted motor could do no more. However, we were prepared for this. Unstrapping the swag of five blankets and the tent fly, we proceeded to spread them out one by one across the sandy waste. The motor roared into life once more and as the back wheel passed over each blanket gave it a sort of little triumphant kick, almost playfully, and passed on to do likewise with the next, until finally the tent fly had its turn leaving six crumpled-up little bundles lying on the sand. Having done that the motor once more decided to rest until we had respread the set-up to commence again.

We repeated this procedure over and over again until we finally reached the opposite bank. How simple it all was. The terrors of the famous Fitzroy were now considerably reduced and we were confident that we could negotiate this mighty crossing after all.

That night we camped at a location where a sign of sorts had been nailed to a tree, pointing lethargically in a general direction towards untracked spinifex and stating 'To Fitzroy'. The direction in which the sign pointed uncertainly was devoid of any obvious tracks, so we scouted around in the gathering dusk, hoping to determine the track to take the next morning. In this we learnt nothing so we adopted our 'when in doubt sleep on it' policy once again.

In the morning there wasn't any breakfast—we had run out of water again—so we took off along the only faint track we could see, which to our suspicious minds was not leading us in the direction we wanted to go. The early sun told us we were going north, but we somehow expected our track to lead us west sooner or later. After some nine miles we found ourselves at a bore, and here the track terminated. We turned around and promptly rode back to our old camp site and the 'To Fitzroy' sign. Eighteen miles of precious petrol had been consumed for nothing. Once more we examined the ground, and finally found the faintest of indications of a track leading west.

12

Sand and Spinifex

THE TOWNSHIP of Fitzroy was located about a mile beyond the river crossing, and as we finally approached the river and looked across the broad expanse of sand, to our great joy we saw several houses standing on the opposite bank. We were back to civilisation again, and our petrol worries would be over as soon as we crossed that expanse of sand. Having carefully studied the best approach we pelted down the steep bank, and with the motor roaring in low gear we hit the water with a great splash. With water hurtling all over us, we got through onto the coarse heavy sand. The motor could do no more so we dismounted and took stock of the position. We offloaded all our gear onto the sand, and once more spreading the tent fly and five blankets out as a runway, we started off again. Shortly, five Aborigines appeared. They took a keen interest in the proceedings but kept their distance, apparently bewildered by what they saw.

We struggled and pushed and finally invited the watchers to join in the fun. They rushed in excitedly, each endeavouring to gain a more advantageous position, and with this extra assistance we kept going until we were safe on the opposite bank. Frank pointed to the tent fly and to each Aborigine, then marched them back to our supplies, which he threw onto the fly. Then he marched them back again like a sergeant major. We gave them the remainder of our niki-niki then rode up to the nearest residence, which fortunately was the Fitzroy Police Station, where a cup of tea was immediately produced.

Leaving the hospitality of the policeman and his wife, we prepared to cover the short distance of perhaps one mile into the township, but suddenly we came upon a delightful little

85

stream which presented itself as an excellent camping spot.

Our shirts and socks had not been washed since leaving Darwin, except when we waded about the various river crossings. And the engine needed an overhaul. So here we stopped, safe in the knowledge that the township was only a short distance away and within easy reach.

It was at this stage that the few inhabitants of the nearby Fitzroy township heard the loud noise of a motor vehicle which most certainly was not a car. So they waited, and waited—for two days. The motor could no longer be heard. Blissfully unaware of this, we were washing our clothes and at peace with the world, caring not for the township which was just to hand. Once again we had not taken into account the strange noises we created as we fought our way through this desolate land and its people.

The townsfolk had heard the motor stop and knowing it was not an aeroplane in trouble and that whoever was responsible for that noise must pass along Fitzroy's one and only street sooner or later, they returned to the bar of the solitary pub and decided to drink it out. There was little else to do in the small frontier town. As I eventually walked out of the silent bush into the sleepy town of Fitzroy, nonchantly swinging an empty petrol can in one hand, little did I know that the whole town had been awaiting my arrival for two days.

The loungers outside the pub rose in a body and advanced towards me. 'Where have you come from?' they asked. And when I told them we had camped at the little creek between town and the river they then told me of the noise of a motor they had heard two days ago. Of course I was astonished to learn Frank and I had thrown the town into a state of expectancy and excitement. That matter now settled I enquired about petrol. We were out of it again, having used our last supplies during the engine overhaul. I bought our usual one case. One case of petrol is two four-gallon cans.

I walked back and told Frank of all the consternation in town. Then we filled up our tanks and reappeared again amongst the townsfolk as an entire unit. Small incidents such

86

as we caused would be something like the circus coming to town in such a remote spot as Fitzroy and my earlier conversation with the locals was gone over once again in minute detail.

The spinifex grass was starting to get us down, for the sidecar wheel beat a steady tattoo, mile after mile, bumping over each individual tuft of grass with regular but frightening monotony.

Spinifex grass grows in tufty clumps about twelve inches in diameter and stands apart from its neighbour in an area of reddish coloured coarse sand. Each clump is about eight inches high.

From time to time the land would change from spinifex-covered to lightly timbered country, where bush grass and the scattered trees presented a veritable fire hazard.

As we motored along we came upon a waterhole which was obviously a watering spot for the semi-wild cattle grazing over this area, and deeply embedded up to its belly in the muddy water was a hopelessly bogged bullock. We promptly dismounted for we needed some of this water, muddy or not, but we decided to pull that bullock out first. Each of us grasped one of the animal's horns and tugged, but it seemed to resent this intrusion upon his meditation. I suppose he had been cogitating in that bog for two or three days already. Now the more we pulled, the more determinedly he resisted

We had a pretty fair idea, of course, that the beast would most likely charge either of us once it was free, and with that in mind we had each in our own way already determined our means of escape. However, this never happened and we needn't have worried unduly over being hurled over the animal's head into the air. We just could not budge that uncooperative bullock, so rather than leave it to a slow lingering death we put a bullet into its brain to end its misery.

Than we filled the billy can with muddy water, strained it several times through a coarse bandage from our medical kit and decided here was the place for the noonday meal.

We adjourned some little distance from the now dead

bullock, lighted a fire and lo!—a puff of wind caught the blaze
and in seconds the surrounding grass was on fire. There was
a narrow cattle pad a short distance away and we raced away
ahead of the fire and lit the grass along the narrow track,
beating it out with our hats and feet until we had formed a fire
break wide enough to prevent the rapidly approaching flames
from escaping into the limitless distance which lay beyond.
We'd have been riding through that fire for days had it escaped
beyond that narrow cattle pad.

Now the fire menace was eliminated we resumed the lunch
break, and while I was busy straining the mud out of the water
through the sling bandage, Frank mixed up the dough for
lunch. Since we had suddenly come upon a plentiful, even if
doubtful, source of water, this meal was to be dumplings. But
when Frank went to add the usual suet fat to the mixture he
found that we had none left. He carried on, however, and
made his dumplings without, rolling them into golfball size,
and dropping them into the muddy boiling water. Then we sat
down and watched them boil for the allotted time of twenty
minutes. At the end of this time we each took our share,
covered them with treacle and sat down to lunch. Our spoons
made no impression on our dumplings and I doubt if even a
knife and fork would penetrate those tough hard balls. We
threw them away, and as they hit the hard ground each little
ball of dough gave a little jump as if elated at escaping dem-
olition. All of which proved that one cannot make dumplings
without fat.

We had nothing else to hand so packed up and left. This
must have been one of the unluckiest days during this holiday
jaunt of ours.

Towards late afternoon to our bewilderment the track suddenly forked into two different directions. One we knew would
lead to the coastal town of Derby, but which one we knew not.
Here we were at a quandary. Petrol supply was of course
always our main concern and we just could not use up this
precious fluid following blind tracks.

When in doubt, either put the billy on and make a cup of

The Margaret
River—using our
blankets to the best
advantage

RIVER CROSSINGS

The Victoria River

The Fitzroy River,
helped by local
Aborigines

MAKING FIRE

The old way . . . (an Aborigine in Central Australia shows us how)

. . . and the new, (cooking the midday meal on the Nullarbor)

tea or sleep on it. So with this motto in mind we decided, in the knowledge that a motor vehicle would be going through to Derby during the night, that we would stay put. To make quite sure we would intercept that vehicle we planted ourselves fair and square the fork in the track. And to make doubly sure we carefully swept each track with bushes so we could determine which track had been used if we slept too soundly during the night.

In these extreme cases one must not be over particular regarding sleeping quarters. Just lie down like a dog in the most convenient place or one might miss out altogether.

At some time during the night I awoke. What caused me to wake up I do not know, for my conscious mind was dead to the world, but on the instant I was out of those blankets in a fully upright position fair in the middle of the track before the truck even came into view, and as the driver swung into view there I was standing full within the glare of headlights waving him down.

What a surprise those two occupants got to see a solitary figure standing there in the lonely bush 30 miles from the township of Derby in the dead of night.

We quickly discovered why the track had forked at this spot. One fork led to Derby while the other fork led to Broome and obviated the necessity to go right into Derby and back again to the spot where we now stood. That is, if we had enough petrol to allow us to take the more direct route to Broome. After due consideration we decided to take the risk and follow the shorter route.

Our first problem now lay in the nature of the track. It soon became very sandy, making heavy going for our outfit and from time to time we would come upon a stretch of country covered once more with one of our biggest hazards—spinifex. These hazards made progress both slow and frustrating and kept the speed down to such a low level that we would drop down to second gear, gain a little speed, then change back to top gear again. This continual gear-changing went on for miles. Now and again the sidecar passenger would vault from his seat and throw his weight behind the outfit to help the motor, or run along behind until the going became easier.

After repairing a troublesome slow-leak puncture we managed to bag four turkeys which ensured several good meals and boosted our spirits considerably. It is wonderful what a good meal, or even a cup of tea, can do under such conditions.

There was a waterhole marked on the map but it failed to materialise and as we urgently needed water we were forced to keep going past sundown. The moon rose and gave sufficient light for us to follow the track but the sand made driving difficult and we could not see far enough ahead to gauge what lay before us. We seemed to push as much as drive.

After an hour or so of this night riding we finally came to a well of water which quite likely was the one shown on our sketchy map. However, the mosquitoes were here in complete command and we hastily filled the water tanks and left the scene as quickly as we could, camping elsewhere for the night.

The following morning we were once more fighting the heavy sand, so much so that we finally decided to forget petrol conservation scheme, just keep going in second gear and resign ourselves to the outcome. If the fuel ran out, it ran out.

Later that morning we came upon another well where we had a much-needed wash and, as mosquitoes were not a real menace, rested a while and examined the petrol position and mileage yet to go. We figured it was another 50 miles to Broome, and much now depended on the general condition of the sandy surface as to whether the petrol would last the distance. A little bit further on we came upon a crudely painted sign which read 'Broome 35M'.

It is difficult to describe the sudden change in one's mental outlook when one receives confirmation that there is only 35 miles to go instead of 50. Our morale was further boosted by an improvement in road conditions. Life was worthwhile again and we immediately fell to telling each other what a wonderful meal we would have when we got to Broome.

13

A Lunch Invitation

BROOME—the very name conjures up visions of adventure. Luggers; pearls; isolation; tough, hard-living Australians dressed in tropical whites and solar topees; Malay pearl divers and Oriental cooks and a mixed collection of all types of island people, black, yellow and brown. And they were all there, just as they had been written about in those adventure stories I had read as a youngster.

The little sea port was built against a backdrop of flat arid land, with nothing to break the monotony except saltbush and spinifex as far as the eye could see. That is how we saw Broome, only in reverse. As we came through that saltbush and spinifex from the north we saw a scattered settlement of houses mixed up strangely with tall poles towering above them. We thought everybody must have installed high radio antennae, but as we drew nearer we discovered the poles were the masts of pearl luggers anchored in a small creek at the back of town, away from the sea.

From our angle of approach from the interior, the luggers came first, then the settlement and then the sea. We found later that the luggers were laid up temporarily and moored in this sheltered creek to escape cyclonic weather, which at certain times of the year batters the north-west coast unmercifully. The little creek haven was further fortified against heavy weather by a thick belt of mangrove swamp, and the conglomerate of mangroves, masts and some houses formed a half circle around the township.

A mile away across the flat uninhabited plain, and standing aloof from this scene, was the main residential area where most of the white population had their homes. The shanty town shops were similar in all respects to those in Darwin, and were also operated by Chinese.

A cosmopolitan crowd of idlers quickly gathered around us as we motored up to the post office to receive our long overdue mail, which by now had travelled halfway around the continent. First to central Queensland in the north, then all the way back to Sydney, west to Perth and north to Broome—a distance of around 7,000 miles.

There was always a moment of relaxation and relief upon entering any town. Communication with the major cities by the telegraph was once again possible, and here we had the opportunity of advising family and friends that we had finally emerged from some desolate area into a safe haven. The folk back home, needless to say, followed our movements as best they could from this infrequent communication. Sometimes we spent three to four weeks between towns of this nature, and back home, all our family and friends knew was that we were somewhere in between. But in what condition, dead, or alive? There was no way of knowing. And so it was that our first place of call in these towns was always the post office.

Upon entry we would immediately be recognised as travellers of some description. Our travel-worn breeches and jackboots, once a beautiful tan in colour, were by now white with wear and dust. Furthermore we wore green fly-veils around our battered felt hats, which for the most part had been sat upon, stamped upon and otherwise ill-treated. The postal clerk would watch and wait until we advanced to the counter with the telegram ready for despatch. He would carefully read it and then would come, as we already expected, the flood of questions. 'Ah! What are the roads like up north?' 'Had many punctures?' 'What are you getting out of this?'

These were quite friendly comments I suppose, but when one has been battling through long sandy stretches, struggling over rock-strewn tracks and eating nothing but dishes concocted of flour and water or whatever fell to our gun, one is not always inclined to extend goodwill and exchange merry banter to one's fellow man. Particularly when from previous experience you know full well what the next question is going to be. So when the clerk got to 'What are the roads like up north?' I looked him square in the eye and said in the most unfriendly manner, 'What bloody roads?'

I hope I may be excused for this, but somewhere, sometime, one has to blow off steam and it is quite frankly far better to do this with a stranger. However, wherever we went we still had the same barrage of more or less set questions and at one stage we thought it might be an idea to print the answers beforehand and display them in a prominent position some-where on the sidebox, for all and sundry to read.

The interior of our sidebox was also a source of wonder and inquisitiveness to the onlookers. They liked our display of armoury; of our boomerangs, the throwing stick which we had found somewhere, and other artefacts we had gathered along the track. In fact, around our lonely camp fire it was always a source of amusement to reminisce on the various portly, well-fed, out-of-condition males who envied us in our style of living. If only they really knew, or were to sample just a few days of it, I think they would have happily scurried back to a life in which Mum had a three-course dinner awaiting them every evening and where they could fraternise with their mates over a few beers in the local pub.

In Broome, several of the older men suggested most strongly that we dine with them at the Roebuck Bay Hotel. With longing thoughts of that long-overdue good meal, we readily agreed, so off we went to the Roebuck Bay hotel and sat at a table with several pearlers and businessmen of the town.

These characters evidently dined here daily, and they knew all the ropes, for as soon as a plate of bread was placed before us it was pounced upon by these regulars. Watching our manners, we waited for the bread plate to be replenished. But once more we were beaten to the punch. Our main dish order was not so much based upon quality as quantity—or did it seem that way because the dinner plates were too small? At any rate, the long anticipated meal was a dismal failure, and we were too ill at ease in these surroundings to ask for more.

Our perpetually shaky financial situation prevented us from staying long in towns, so soft beds and good meals were not for us. The great open spaces were more in our line and having done all we had to do in Broome, and seen all there was to see, we asked for directions that would set us on the road to Perth.

We were advised to leave town by the track we had entered upon, until we reached a gate about thirteen miles out, and there turn right. This sounded easy, but one bright local thought that maybe we had entered town by a different track, and so decided to personally see that we were headed south. As we came to the thirteen-mile gate he was already there, holding it open for us to pass through, and with a farewell shout of 'good luck' he turned his car around and we sped on. Relieved to know that we headed in the right direction, we felt most grateful for the thoughtfulness and hospitality shown by this fellow Aussie who had undertaken a round trip of 26 miles on our behalf.

14

Drinks With a Boxing Cat

THE WORST OF our journey was now over and we were already
past the halfway mark. The track showed a marked improvement, due no doubt to there being more travellers leaving
Perth and going north, and we were able to cover many more
miles each day. Nevertheless it was still rare to encounter
anybody else on the road during the day. We were still over
1,000 miles from Perth and the beating the machine and
sidebox had taken across that formidable stretch from Darwin
must eventually take its toll. On top of everything, our money
was getting very low. For all that, we now felt that we were
back in civilization at last.

We were also moving out of cattle country and into sheep
country. The evidence of this was the number of gates which
had to be opened and closed as the track passed through the
various holdings dotted along our route.

About 30 miles out of Broome we made camp at a well
shown on our map, but we were not the only people who had
elected to camp where water was available. A family of sandalwood gatherers had also made camp there and as we settled
in the father and son sauntered over and settled down for a
long yarn. Since they had journeyed from the south, and we
from the north, we were soon exchanging our respective views
of the difficulties that lay ahead of each party.

During this conversation, father and son carefully watched
as we went about in a nonchalant manner, preparing the
evening meal. They watched as we took a handful of flour and
placed it in the mixing bowl, watched as one of us rummaged
about in the sidebox and finally produced a piece of rubber
tubing and, sucking at one end with the other end dropped

into the top of the water tank, siphoned off sufficient for our needs and mixed up the dough.

The conversation never stopped while we cooked our flap-jack slowly in the bottom of the frying pan until it was done on both sides then spread treacle upon our half of the flapjack. That was that. Being temporarily out of tea, we wiped the back of our hands across our mouths in lieu of serviettes and the meal was over.

One does not necessarily invite guests to dine on occasions such as this and our guests apparently were too polite to express any opinion on our culinary arts, or the frugality of our meal. However, they also must have been impressed by the dextrous manner in which it was so quickly prepared—and devoured.

The mother and daughters of the northward-bound family were over at their camp, busily and hastily writing letters, for here was an excellent opportunity to have them swiftly on their way. They would hand them over to us to post at the railhead in Meekatharra when we got there.

Conversation of course always led around to the tribal, nomadic natives of the far north, and as we discussed this subject with the sandalwood gatherers, the son who had been out that very day with Major, their native assistant, told of how he had said at noonday, 'No tea today, Major, no bloody matches'. Major thereupon quickly split a small piece of wood, inserted some dry spinifex grass in the split, and sawed rapidly across the top with another stick until sparks fell on the grass. He then removed the grass and blew gently on it until it burst into flame. As simple as that—nothing to it. And to prove the point the young fellow went over to his camp and returned with those sticks. We sawed and sawed, each in his turn, but could not even raise smoke, and decided that Major was a better man than we were.

We were always astir at dawn and with such scanty fare as we had, breakfast was quickly disposed of and we were up and away before our neighbours were aware of it. But they at least knew their letters were on their way, and that really was something.

96

About noon we arrived at Lagrange, a tiny telegraph station on the north–south telegraph line linking Broome with Perth. Here we met a retired telegraph operator who had elected to remain put, even after he had vacated the position as operator. He continued to live in the area with his wife—an Aboriginal full-blood. They had two daughters who were away 'going walkabout' with the rest of the tribe. The old gentleman had originally come from Sydney and was most pleased to reminisce over his early life there. He had not seen his home for many years and we were invited to stay for the midday meal.

Since we had not eaten particularly well with our pearler friends at Broome, or since, we readily accepted the invitation to dine here in the little shack. The sumptuous meal of boiled goat, flour dumplings and tomatoes served as a casserole was absolutely delicious.

The good lady of the house could not speak our language and we could not speak hers, so we could only bow and gesture our thanks for such a fine meal as we departed.

Homesteads were much closer to each other now and later in that same afternoon we came to Anna Plains. Here we handed over the mail entrusted to us by the postmaster at Broome. The station's bookkeeper was pleased to receive it so expeditiously and asked if there was anything we needed. Yes, we needed flour. Our flour tin, which held about three pounds, was filled for us. As was our usual custom we inquired, 'How much would that be?' and to our astonishment were told 'Three shillings'.

He was either an excellent bookkeeper or he urgently needed three shillings. This had been the only time on our long journey we paid for what were known as 'station hand-outs', and as we parted with the money we secretly wished we had never delivered the mail in the first place. Then we pumped up the leaky back tyre and took our departure.

We entered once more upon plain, open country, entirely devoid of trees. Nothing but spinifex and saltbush. Nothing as far as the eye could see, and away in the far distance, as straight as a gun barrel, we could still discern the track with not so much as a waver or slightest diversion to break the monotony. This went on for several days. To get some interest from the day's work we fell to watching the lizards basking in the sun along the track. One of us would sight a lizard some distance up ahead and as the front wheel bore down upon the reptile it would seemingly disappear. Where it went to we never could determine. We broke the silence from time to time to wonder about this strange thing. Did the lizard burrow into the sand, or did it shoot out to one side? Whatever the explanation, this provided some diversion from riding from one point into the distance and, once we arrived there, repeating the process. We were on the dreaded 'Madman's Track', bordering the western fringes of the Great Sandy Desert.

This went on and on. We were always on the lookout for some signs of trees, without which we had nothing to make a fire for the night's camp and the cooking of the three shillings worth of newly acquired flour. The evenings were also becoming decidedly cooler as we headed south. When darkness finally forced us to call it a day we pulled off the track amidst the clumpy, spiky, spinifex grass and saltbush. There was not a vestige of fire material, and since we could not make a meal of raw flour we simply lay down where we were and slept like homeless dogs.

One morning we looked for a pinhole puncture in the leaky tyre, but without water to show us the air bubble we could not find it. So, putting all the temporary sleeves back in the tyre, each one covering a wall fracture in the canvas wall lining, we placed the leaky tube back in the tyre, pumped the tyre up once more and continued on our way. Fortunately the much-used hand pump never faltered at any time and just as well. We had no spares for hand pumps. We had travelled on just one mile when the tyre blew out with a loud bang. There was no further need to look for a slow leak. We now had a much larger one and we put our last remaining spare tube in, replaced the seven sleeves once again over the seven fractures, and departed.

Many lives have been lost over this dry waterless expanse of

track of just on 100 miles of desert, and we had crossed this
area entirely ignorant of its dangers in this respect. Perhaps
there are times when in one's life when ignorance is bless.

Port Hedland was our next objective but upon arrival at The
Coongan, a small hotel 25 miles from Port Hedland we were
told that it was not necessary to go to that town, as Perth lay
directly ahead. 'The Port' lay on a spur line in to the coast and
it would be therefore necessary to retrace our tracks and return
to The Coongan. The hotel proprietor meanwhile suggested
we might have a drink with him. He later suggested we have
a drink with his wife, and some time later we also had a drink
with his boxing cat as well as drinking with various other
objects of less material value. Several hours later and unsure
of anything anymore except that we were not going to Port
Hedland, we steered an unsteady course for our machine and
made an equally unsteady departure from The Coongan, laden
with eggs and tomatoes presented to us by our host's good
lady. The beverages had also filled us with a spirit of goodwill.

This was indeed a most pleasant day and we sped on in
happy spirit. But I'm afraid that we had tarried too long and
had drunk too many toasts to almost everything in sight. We
were almost to the point of breaking into song as our motor
roared an accompaniment and the wind rushed pleasantly past
our happy faces. Life was really worth living. Presently,
however, we became aware of a small stream swiftly flowing
across our path. It was too late to do much about it and we
hit that water with hardly any reduction in speed.

Frank, whose turn it was in the driving seat, simply decided
to ignore the stream and hit the running water with enough
abandon to throw up a shower of water which drenched everything in the sidebox, including myself.

Due to the benevolence of our hosts we were in such a happy
state of well-being that we totally ignored the present problem
of water-soaked clothing and my bedraggled appearance and
simply burst into laughter. In fact we were almost tempted to
repeat this hilarious performance, it was such a happy
interlude.

We were within easy reach of the little mining town of Marble Bar and we decided that come what may we would pass right on through that town and camp on the other side, thus escaping any further invitation to drink toasts to this and that. Marble Bar always did carry the reputation of being one of the thirtiest places on God's Earth.

The sight of a horde of wild goats prompted us to seek the opportunity of adding meat to our menu. There was also a bounty of sixpence a head on wild goats in Western Australia, and bounties were always on our minds. We could use them to supplement our slender purse, so we knew almost every bounty there was in existence. But anything to eat other than the inevitable flour and water took precedence and here was an unlimited source of meat.

Frank took the shotgun from its resting place and crouchingly approached the herd, while in the background I shouted slurringly, 'It's not loaded, you fool'. Frank took no notice whatsoever and continued to stalk what I had long-since regarded as a black stump, when suddenly there was a loud bang and the whole herd fled. The black stump went with them. Apparently Frank had a ball cartridge in his pocket. Had that ball hit my black stump it would have thrown strips of meat all over the place but Frank was in no position to hit anything—and nor was I.

However, we still had our tomatoes and eggs as well as our flour, so we lit a fire, cooked our delicate provisions, relaxed and took life easily.

Finally we decided we had better get moving and pass through Marble Bar before nightfall. Some five miles out from this remote town we came to a gate across the track being held open courteously for us by a man. His car was standing by, facing towards The Coongan.

We waved greetings, thanked the man for his courtesy but did not stop. A moment later I glanced over my shoulder and saw the car following us. This seemed a strange thing to do and I remarked on this to Frank.

It was only a day or two later that it dawned on us that the good lady of the Coongan Hotel must have phoned ahead to Marble Bar to advise that two motorcyclists had left her hotel after imbibing with her husband to such an extent that maybe it would be wise to send someone out to meet us if we did not arrive within a reasonable time. We in the meantime were enjoying ourselves in our merry state, and were leisurely taking our own time.

We guessed that the townsfolk had got tired of waiting for us and had despatched one of their number to see what had happened to us. Marble Bar had apparently cooled its heels while we chased goats, rode madly through watercourses, cooked eggs and tomatoes and generally frittered away a very pleasant afternoon.

At Marble Bar they were all awaiting our arrival in front of the hotel and we duly acknowledged their welcome. Nobody said a word to us about the delay, but sensing further trouble and possibly more boxing cats, we tarried not and sought safer surroundings in the vast countryside on the other side of town. As Marble Bar is reputedly the hottest town in Australia, any excuse is as good as another to combat this heat in the pleasant atmosphere of the pub.

Despite the distractions we had covered 153 miles by the time we made camp, and the next day covered an additional 180 miles in ten hours. During the course of this day we saw two men approaching us on foot, carrying nothing but water and a shotgun. They had no cartridges for the gun, and as we stopped to ask about road conditions ahead we learned that their swags were being carried on a following donkey cart being driven to Marble Bar by an old-timer who had as passengers on his cart an Aboriginal man and his lubra. Obviously a man of discretion, he also had the cartridges for the shotgun.

Our hiking friends begged us for a 12-gauge cartridge or two, but upon hearing of their cartridges being withheld by the donkey-cart driver we decided not to cooperate. Maybe, as they said, they only wanted to shoot a sheep for food but even that was apparently not allowed. Several miles further on we

101

came upon the donkey cart and its occupants, just as they had told us.

This is very uninteresting country, except perhaps for a geologist. Day after day, mile after mile, we passed through what is locally known as 'breakaway country'—low ridgy hills and rocky outcrops with scant vegetation. This monotony started to get us down. We were passing through mining country somewhat similar to that encountered around Mount Isa and Cloncurry on the opposite side of the continent.

However, day after day we were bearing down on Perth at the rate of about 160 miles a day. This was nearly double the daily mileage on our journey north to Darwin. When we were within two miles of the small mining town of Nanning darkness was getting close, but we were anxious to pass through the township and find a suitable camp site. The nights had become bitterly cold as we proceeded south. It was still August and the tail end of winter.

As we approached the little township Frank remarked, 'There's a man lying down over there on that gibber plain'. His horse was standing by, so we quickly dismounted and walked over amongst the scattered rocks to determine the trouble. He had obviously been thrown onto his head amongst these boulders, as there were two gaping wounds on his skull. We thought him to be dead with such terrible head wounds, but as we investigated he muttered incoherently.

We bound his wounds with bandages from our medical kit and lost no time in riding into town to report our find. As we had done everything possible by at least preventing his lying out all night on that cold gibber plain, we continued on our way in search of our camp site before darkness really set in.

We never did hear the result of this episode as, in accordance with usual procedure, we hurried on our southward journey towards Meekatharra and Perth.

15

The Civic Reception

WE WERE GETTING well south again. The nights were growing colder and we were never totally warm, not even with five blankets and a groundsheet, and we were always driven out and astir at dawn, only too anxious to get the fire going again from the night's hot embers. Eventually, we only had a few hours ride to reach Meekatharra, the rail head linking the far north of Western Australia with Perth, 600 miles to the south.

Once again we sent telegrams back home to announce our arrival. We were now within easier reach of civilisation and even if the motorcycle fell to pieces entirely we were assured of being able to get home by rail. But we were still under motor power, even if we were holding things together with Cobb & Co. hitches made from fencing wire, with sundry 'U' bolts, plates and other makeshift gadgets preventing the sidecar chassis from cracking up altogether, not to mention all the sleeves in the back tyre and the cracked front forks. We had also thrown two tyres away. To all outward appearances they looked quite good, except that each had one neat cut made by a sharp stone which was enough to render it useless. But we had our tins of flour and of treacle.

More importantly, there lay the job ahead—to be the first to take a motorcycle and sidecar outfit around the continent, touching at all capital cities. This was our goal, and however long it was to take didn't matter. This was enough to later on get us listed in *The Guiness Book of World Records*. The fact that we also broke the fastest time recorded for this journey—except by air—was beside the point. We still had to ride this rattletrap conveyance along over a further 3,000 miles.

Upon presentation of our telegrams for despatch at Meek-atharra, the postal official there proceeded to fire the usual questions at us. 'Is this an advertising stunt,' he asked, 'or just for pleasure?' And the answer to that question was really simple—just pleasure. Can you imagine a better way to thoroughly enjoy yourself? Night after night sleeping on the hard cold ground trying to keep your hipbone located in the hip hole you had dug in the ground; sharing the five blankets to try to keep warm under an open sky; drinking muddy water from waterholes; bouncing up and down all day from daylight till dark over spinifex clumps, or rocks; existing on meagre fare and often relying on skill with the rifle to supplement the diet.

There's nothing like a quick jaunt around Australia on a motorcycle to try you out.

We were now well into the mineral bearing areas of Western Australia, and every small town was a mining centre. The country was desolate, uninteresting, and devoid of stimulating characteristics. We continually found ourselves on long stretches of road with nothing whatever to look at except salt-bush. However, the mining townships were reasonably close together and it always became our objective to try and pass through one early enough in the afternoon to allow us to make camp before entering the next town. We were getting very short of money and could not possibly afford to be caught in town at nightfall.

As we drove into the slightly larger town of Mount Magnet we were acclaimed by a tall, uniformed gentleman who was a postal inspector and he, together with the local doctor, decided that we should have our thirst quenched in a nearby hotel. Although we really could not afford to imbibe freely in hotels, these two gentlemen considered it an honour, and indeed a duty, to buy us 'one for the road'.

The 'one' led to another, and then a third and so on. I lost count after about the fourth, and all I remember clearly beyond that was that the doctor and the postal gentleman become embroiled in bitter argument—whether the postal gentleman disagreed upon some medical matter, or the doctor disagreed upon some postal one I do not know. I suppose Mary the barmaid was the only one who did know, but I never did get to ask her because around this stage the party broke up and we took a very unsteady departure, leaving the doctor and the postal gentleman to their own devices.

Clouds began to fill the sky for the first time since leaving New South Wales and it looked like rain before morning. So as we camped that evening we rigged up the tent fly, thrown over two sticks poked here and there into the framework of our machine, thus making a crude shelter about three feet high and under which we crawled to lie down upon our blankets. This was the first time in two months that we had not slept under the stars.

During the night there was a rain shower pattering down upon the makeshift shelter and we were forced to get out and scratch a small trench around us to direct the water clear of the sleeping area before once more returning to our blankets.

We had a good sleep, despite the rain, and for once did not have to hurry away at dawn for we were within easy reach of the city of Perth and we had to clean ourselves up in order to present a reasonably civilized appearance in the city of my birth. We had 32 miles to go.

This was the Perth centenary year and the Centenary Committee had decided they were not going to allow our arrival into their fair city to pass unnoticed. They had therefore organised a welcoming party to mark the occasion of our visit.

Needless to say there were many repairs to be carried out here in Perth before the final dash across the great Nullarbor Plain on the third, and last, phase of our journey. We had always referred to this journey in terms of phases. The first, Sydney to Darwin, was approximately 3,000 miles; the second, Darwin to Perth, by far the most hazardous and of about the same distance. Perth to Sydney was a slightly shorter distance, and far less hazardous. On this last phase we would pass through two other major cities, Adelaide and Melbourne, as well as quite a number of large towns.

We received telegrams from various motoring bodies congratulating us on our achievement to date, and the Harley-Davidson agent urged us to complete the journey without delay. It was obvious now that we would not only finish the project, but that we were also well ahead of the previous motoring record time. The agent suggested that since we could now easily break the speed record we might as well go for it as well, which would set a greater challenge for others to better, be it by car or motorcycle.

We now began to take a different view of the position generally. Why not have two records instead of one? And with that thought in mind we set about overhauling the outfit to enable us to do just that.

Due to our success to date, we now had a certain amount of cooperation from various people from the motoring world, and one gentleman invited us to his home and to the use of his garage where we could work in relative comfort and privacy. We, in the meantime, had told each other that we didn't care too much for all the handshaking and questioning we received in organised gatherings, and had decided we would leave Perth when we were ready to go, quite unostentatiously.

Our appearance around Perth created some attention, however—mainly, I suppose, because of our dusty, worn, riding clothes, and being identically dressed. We were forever being besieged by curious people asking those interminable but to us predictable questions. We were not used to crowds. Half a dozen Aborigines were sufficient people in one group for us, and they didn't ask 'What are you getting out of this?' or 'How are the roads up North?'

However, our sneaky escape from Perth was not to be. We were taken in hand by the Civic Fathers, speedily transported around the city, and generally very well looked after. In between times we worked on our machine, and that took two or three days.

When the day for departure arrived, we were advised to be at the General Post Office in busy Forrest Place by 10.30 a.m.

We rode up on our battered looking outfit clad in our

long-suffering riding clothes. Leather breeches were tucked into the tops of our riding boots, all of which now showed the stress of wear. Instead of having that nice new shiny look of polished leather, they were drab and grey. Our medium-length riding coats were still in good condition, except for that gash in the right sleeve of each coat, which had been covered with a piece of adhesive tape like some badge of distinction or elevated rank.

We managed to park our dejected looking machine and ventured towards the post office steps, at the top of which stood six members of the Perth Centenary Committee, all soberly dress in smart business suits, who advanced towards us and shook our hands one by one with a certain amount of vigour. Then we took up our position in a line with these gentlemen, in somewhat military fashion.

A light drizzle had commenced, and we had therefore been forced to wear our best hats. These were of the slouch felt variety and had been lying around in the bottom of the sidebox, kicked and sat upon for weeks on end.

The faded green fly veils adorning the hatband still maintained their position and, together with the rest of our travelling ensemble, made us look like twins—twin hobos. The throng of people passing along Forrest Place paused and looked—then looked again, and mildly wondered why such a strange-looking pair should be standing as if they belonged in the society of obviously well-dressed businessmen.

But these men had affairs of state to attend to for their city had reached the century mark, and not a stone was to be left unturned in this significant year. We apparently had been considered to be one of those stones.

The onlookers multiplied rapidly, sensing that some alteration to their daily routine was about to be revealed, and gathered around the bottom steps. As their numbers grew they flowed right across Forrest Place and, in overflowing, started to lean out of windows of the buildings opposite. Heads popped out of all vantage places as I gazed awe-stricken upon the scene.

Perth, in the vicinity of Forrest Place, had found a new diversion.

These were the days when public address systems were only being thought of. Our committee had as yet not acquired one, so lifting his voice to a practised pitch the Chairman rose to the occasion and said: 'We have here today, standing in our midst, two young men, who, thinking to see Perth in the year of its centenary have left Sydney, and taken a short cut by way of Darwin'. Of course that 'short cut' was some 7,000 miles longer than the direct route. He then went on to say, 'We admire their courage. We admire their pluck.' Somewhere down there in the crowd someone suggested three cheers, and three hearty cheers rent the air.

The Chairman, thus encouraged, went on to say, 'Now my friend, the Speaker in the House, would also like to say a few words' and Mr Speaker, not to be outdone, said his few words, then handed over to the next gentleman along the line. Eventually each man on the Committee had his say.

We just stood there, like actors in the Scarecrow Scene from *The Wizard of Oz*, wishing we were away somewhere on the Nullarbor Plain, or even that we had perished back along the Madman's Track! And all the time our mute and downtrodden piece of machinery, our modus operandi, stood quietly down there near the bottom step, surrounded and gazed upon by the crowd.

It was becoming fairly obvious from much whispering and shuffling amongst the Committee that they were sparring for time, and I heard one of them say, 'Where's the Lord Mayor?' Then next, to my great astonishment I distinctly heard the words, 'Perhaps one of the boys would like to say a few words'.

I wondered what on earth would give anybody that strange idea. All we wanted to do was escape, but that was impossible. We were hemmed in. Two humbler, homeless dogs such as we had never graced Perth's Forrest Place in the hundred years of its existence. I sneaked a quick look at Frank from under the battered brim of my hat. He hadn't turned a muscle. Frank's like that. He doesn't turn muscles unless in hot pursuit of a kangaroo joey, and then the thought dawned on me that I had been born here—I was one of them—a Sandgroper.

Here was my cue, so I up and told the entire throng. This news evidently touched the heartstrings of several old Sandgroper ladies who, having by now mounted the steps to our podium level, insisted on kissing us both. While this unseemly conduct was being pursued, an inebriated gentleman, also evidently carried away by the momentous occasion, and not wishing to be outdone by the fairer sex, took us by the hand and muttered incoherent words with a beer-laden breath.

Not having the power of oratory equal to our friends of the Committee, I did not go into any details other than to thank them all for this astonishing display of encouragement.

When it became apparent that the Lord Mayor had still not arrived, we decided it was time to move on. But we still had that large crowd to contend with. We fought and struggled, but all to no avail. There were more elderly ladies, and more drunks, and we were at their mercy. There were no young ones. Finally a policeman came to our assistance and we ultimately gained the slender protection of our machine.

Presently, however, there appeared a further commotion up along Forrest Place. Heads began to look about in unruly fashion; policemen's helmets could be seen moving quickly from here to there. The crowd then fell away and revealed the somewhat portly figure of the Lord Mayor bearing down on us. He was running late, and his fellow orators had by now had their say and possibly gone their separate ways. However, according to the daily press: 'His Worship led the large crowd in three hearty cheers for the young adventurers'.

Eventually, and with the assistance of Perth's police officers, we were ready to regain our freedom on the open road. The numbers of people were still swelling, and it appeared that the latecomers were all anxious to know just what was going on. We all seem to need to know just what it was that have missed out on. After some time more policemen's helmets could be seen bobbing about on the outskirts of the crowd and we were relieved to see a break in the crowd wide enough to drive through and we were off.

The rain had increased to a steady drizzle, but it would have taken far more than a rainstorm to stop us now.

That night far, far from Perth, we were once more camped under the stars, and for once we could even dispense with the flour and treacle diet. We had been able to buy meat and vegetables, sugar and tea in an ordinary civilised manner.

Around the camp fire that night, with our stomachs comfortably fully, and away from that crowd, amongst the denizens of the bushland surroundings, the dingoes and the foxes, the stillness of the night was broken by the sound of voices. We were practising speech-making. 'We have here, today, two young men,' etc., etc.

We had the world to ourselves once more, and it pleased us to recite choice comments from the various speeches made earlier that morning which had either amused us or appealed to our vanity.

16

Across the Nullarbor

WE HAD STARTED out from Sydney with our faces pointing to the north until we reached Darwin, then we turned west for 1,000 miles, then south until we arrived at Perth. Now here we were facing east for the final leg of our journey, but we still had well over 2,000 miles to go.

Day after day we would have the early morning sun in our faces, and by the time it was overhead we would halt for lunch then change places in the driver's seat and carry on until the sun began to dip down on the western horizon behind us. Then we would cast about us for a likely camp site.

The congratulatory telegrams we had received in Perth goaded us on to renewed efforts and we decided that since we were now facing home nothing could stop us. We would ride, run, or even walk, but home we would go. Now our aim for a day's ride would be 200 miles, which doubled the average we'd maintained over the previous 7,000 miles.

With that thought in our minds we made an earlier start each day and a later finish, doggedly riding on until nightfall. Had we been equipped with lights, other than the little hand torch, we would have continued on even after dark . . . and probably have become lost.

In my boyhood days my mother would quite often buy a pair of rabbits from the travelling rabbit-oh for two shillings and sixpence a pair. In those days rabbits became a favourite dish, either baked or stewed. There were rabbits everywhere, and in the west of the state and throughout the country areas they had reached plague proportions. It was not until the introduction of the disease myxomatosis some years later that the rabbit became a rarity. But now, as we entered the grassed area of southern Western Australia we were surprised to see once again the presence of the lowly rabbit. Here would be a change from our daily fare, for a stewed rabbit is a delicious dish.

The rabbits seemed to be as astonished at our appearance as did the natives in the north. They just sat up and looked, which proved to be their undoing. We just sat up and looked back at them along the barrel of the shotgun. We were once again in the land of plenty.

The roads from the outskirts of Perth's eastern suburbs were a great improvement on those to the north. The countryside was beautiful with lush green grass, and the landscape reasonably level and tree-clad in a parklike manner. The rabbits also added to the general scene and in this serene environment we were happy.

The towns were reasonably close together after leaving Perth and we were assured of a steady supply of our meagre necessities until we reached Coolgardie. Here the road branched into two. One way led to Kalgoorlie while the other carried on through a few remote towns to approach the western edge of the Nullarbor Plain. Between Perth and Coolgardie we were able to buy meat and bread. However, our finances were at such low ebb that we had to abstain from such luxuries as were available.

We stopped at a little store in Coolgardie to fill up with fuel and the usual crowd began to gather around us. Amongst them were two elderly Aborigines whose eyes gleamed with delight at the two boomerangs adorning the interior of the sidebox. One native carefully examined the workmanship of the weapon, then tested it for balance much as a white man might squint along the barrel of a rifle, and upon being told the boomerang came from the Kimberleys, he passed it over to his companion with the remark, 'Boomerang belonga Kimberley'. What their final judgment on the workmanship of the Kimberley natives was, they never did say, although by the excited manner in which they passed the weapon from one to the other I would say that it passed as satisfactory at the very least. These boomerangs are not the same weapon we would generally buy at the wayside shop. They are war boomerangs, big and heavy

112

OUTBACK SCENES

Wild turkeys, enough
for several meals

A baby kangaroo
near Wyndham,
northern Australia

Below right: Bottle
tree, Western
Australia

A lonely grave

Fitting the new
sidecar wheel

The all-too-usual
meal of damper and
treacle, Nullarbor
Plain

Overlooking Eucla, at
the border of South
and Western
Australia

We arrive in Perth

Outside Lamroc's at Adelaide, with a speed as well as an endurance record well within our grasp

A triumphant return home after eleven weeks on the road

enough to kill a man, and they do not return when thrown.

We had no reason to stay in Coolgardie, so once we had bought the necessities and filled the petrol tanks we said goodbye to closer settlement and settled down to a long lonely run of many hundreds of miles until we had crossed the great Nullarbor Plain.

In fact Frank and I were more at ease when we knew we had great distances before us. Perhaps this was because of the challenge confronting us, or were we becoming part of the landscape of this great wilderness? We certainly were living like Aborigines for the greater part of the time, and with little to worry us apart from the mechanics of our motorcycle, life was really quite pleasant in the main.

Each day brought something different to break the monotony, even if only a change of scenery. Generally we had better information regarding what lay ahead on the final phase of our journey. The track across the Nullarbor was much better known to motorists than the nonexistent roads of the north, and so it was no great surprise to us to find ourselves atop the Madura Pass—a narrow and rough defile leading from the plateau down almost to sea level.

To our astonishment here we found two men struggling to coax their derelict motor truck to gain the summit, and since there was room for one vehicle only on this rock-strewn narrow pass it necessitated some action on our part to fall in beside these two strangers and assist in pushing their vehicle so we could then make the descent. These men were also able to fill us in on general conditions confronting us across the Nullarbor.

We found no difficulty in descending the Pass and duly arrived at Madura sheep station where we enquired which of the many tracks radiating from the homestead was the one we were to take to the old telegraph relay station of Eucla—now long since out of use. The track from Madura to Eucla extended flat and straight as far as the eye could see. Country like this became a virtual speed track and we peeled the miles off hour after hour.

113

However, come nightfall we found our speedway entirely devoid of wood and we had nothing with which to cook the flour and water or to boil our rabbits. Not only that, but nights across the Nullarbor were bitterly cold and here we were almost reduced to tears with the prospect of no food and scant warmth for the entire night.

Dusk fell and still no trees appeared on our horizon so we rode on cautiously through the darkness until we found ourselves approaching a homestead shown on our map.

We didn't fancy the idea of arriving at a homestead in the dark of night in a motorcycle outfit which carried no lights, as we would certainly have been regarded with some suspicion, so we camped that night amongst the spinifex grass and saltbush. Cold and hungry, we rigged up the tent fly to try to keep out the cold sea breeze as best we could, then crawled beneath the primitive shelter, boots and all, with our balaclavas on. We looked forward to the dawn and another day. In fact it couldn't come soon enough.

In future, we vowed, we would 'stay put' at any timbered country regardless of the day's mileage towards the close of each day.

I have never spent such a miserable night and we were up and away before the crack of dawn, riding hell-bent for timbered country so we could start a fire and cook our damper at least. We had handkerchiefs tied over the lower part of our faces in addition to our balaclavas to help minimise the biting cold. Within two miles we came to Mundrabilla homestead, which we had carefully avoided the previous night. We had not realised we were so close.

Early as we were, we found we were not the only ones astir as the homestead occupants rushed out to see what on earth was making such a noise at such an ungodly hour. They had probably heard our motor on the previous evening, and wondered what could make such an infernal noise and then suddenly cease. We never seemed to fully realise that the noise of our engine could be heard for several miles in flat, barren country. There was simply nothing to absorb it except the low spiky spinifex. In fact these lonely people who spent most of their lives in isolation would generally be only too pleased to have visitors, even if daylight had merged into darkness. However, to our city-bred way of thinking, it was not the proper thing to do to drive up unannounced and simply say, 'Well, here we are. Can you give us a meal and bed for the night?'

Like two masked bandits we sped past the homestead, leaving the onlookers still wondering what on earth was going on, and why hadn't we at least paused long enough to say 'Goodday'! Little did they know that all we were seeking in our haste was a little firewood so we could eat our first meal since lunch the previous day.

We had not gone more than 300 yards past these bewildered people and were still within earshot when our motor coughed, spluttered and gave out altogether. That sound was a familiar one to our practised ears and we knew the main tank was empty, so quickly dismounting we siphoned petrol from the spare tank, refilled the empty one, and sped on once more in a cloud of dust. Finally we came upon some scattered fallen timber, but by this time we had forgotten our hunger and did not stop. We were anxious to reach the disbanded relay station town of Eucla and towards midday saw white sand in the far distance. Beyond this we could see the ocean and knew this would be Eucla.

At least there would be still one inhabitant stationed at the derelict town which had once been a telecommunication post for the relaying of information from the eastern states to the west, and vice versa. And somewhere to the north of Eucla on the great Nullarbor was the Transcontinental Railway which had been instrumental in the closing down of the Eucla Relay Station.

Since we were now on the home stretch, complacency was perhaps beginning to overshadow commonsense and the lesson we had learnt by retiring foodless the previous evening was forcibly brought to our attention. There were to be four or five more days and nights before we had crossed this great treeless desert—flat, low and devoid of vegetation except spinifex grass. Even the natives avoided the place and consequently it appeared that we were the only humans foolish enough to be there.

However, we had entered the western perimeter, and now there was to be no turning back. We would once again ride that speedo around to the point of no return and then calculate the miles, one by one, until we reached the eastern perimeter—and civilisation once again.

At one time a small town had evolved at a point on the coastline at the southern edge of the Nullarbor, following the establishment of the telegraph relay station at Eucla. But as science progressed and radio became more widespread, and progress in telecommunication gathered pace, Eucla became a ghost town. Upon our arrival, there remained but one family, located amongst the derelict homes now half-covered by wind-blown sand. Here we replenished our fuel supply, had a brief chat with the sole inhabitants and sped on our way once more.

The firm level sandy track continued as a veritable speedway and we simply ate up the miles for hour upon hour. Shortly after leaving Eucla we climbed a pass similar to the one we had descended at Madura. Now we would continue to cross the Nullarbor on a higher plateau for a further 500 or 600 miles until we reached the little towns of Ceduna and Penong in South Australia. By then our troubles would be over, or so we imagined. However, it is not always the presence of towns and civilisation that ends one's troubles and we very nearly wrote 'finis' to the whole escapade when we were in more hospitable territory.

Eighteen miles from Eucla our map indicated a well and here we had a long-delayed and frugal meal—our first in 24 hours. According to the map we also had a stretch of heavy sand to cross somewhere between here and Ceduna, but we were not unduly concerned about what the map said because it could not possibly be worse than we had already experienced in the north.

Having eaten our meal we reluctantly left the timbered patch

of country behind and again found ourselves on stretch of tim-
berless plain. The prospect of another cold, sleepless and
hungry night was a depressing one.

We rode on for hours and still came across no signs of firewood, but at dusk we sighted a clump of stunted dead trees
sparsely scattered over the plain. We did not even have to
discuss the issue, but rode amongst those dead trees and felt
a moment of relief just as any other traveller might do as he
drops his travel bags in front of the reception desk in an inter-
national hotel. Dismounting, we found we could quite easily
push these trees over and quickly gathered enough firewood to
ensure a good night's accommodation and the means to cook
a meal.

Man does not necessarily have to be accommodated in a fine
hotel to be comfortable and at peace with the world. To the
contrary, just give him a reasonable amount of firewood, a few
blankets, some flour and water, and above all a box of matches.
Pile these few 'luxuries' in the middle of the Nullarbor and
there you have all you need, even if only for a day or two.
Simplicity is really all we should seek.

During the four days spent in crossing the Nullarbor we saw
no one, except that one lonely family at Eucla and the startled
homesteaders at Mundrabilla. Over the distance of 1,000 miles
it was as if we were the sole human inhabitants of the earth
and we became attuned to this form of existence, blending in
with the harsh surroundings and marvelling at what we saw.
We would possibly open up a conversation at lunchtime over
the lizard that scurried away and totally disappeared before our
very eyes; or upon that magnificent dance display performed
by a flock of brolgas; or on how we very nearly collected a
wayward galah seeking to regain the flock by making a suicidal
attempt to cross our path. There were a thousand and one
things during the day's viewing to absorb the mind, in addition
to a thought now and again about our own well-being. A dingo
track in the sandy waste under the front wheel would be com-
mented upon, or a goanna raising itself on those peculiar front
legs that made it look like hydrofoil raised upon its foils as it

streaked for the nearest tree in which to seek refuge, always spiralling to ensure the tree trunk was between it and the human invader. All these things we observed as we went our way, and were the prime subjects of conversation at stopping time.

About midday one day we came upon the area marked on the map as 'Heavy Sand', but to our great relief we found no difficulty whatever in getting through. The family of sandal-wood gatherers we had met in the north-west had advised us to avoid this area, known as the Yardea Sands, by taking a different and much longer route, but we figured the place could not be any worse those we had already battled with when crossing the terrible river beds of the Margaret, the Louise and the Fitzroy Rivers.

We then passed through a small station property and drove right around the homestead in an endeavour to discover which of the numerous tracks leading from it would take us to Fowlers Bay. Coming upon a telegraph line we figured this must surely lead to our next port of call. However, as no track was plainly visible other than a clearing following the line of poles, we held council and determined to follow the telegraph line. We were by now sorry we had not stopped at the home-stead to make enquiries, but that would have necessitated a delay of perhaps several hours as we explained where we had been and where we were going, etc., etc.

Later, we found ourselves on a well-beaten track which soon led to a small road sign which read 'To Penong'. So to Penong we went, bypassing Fowlers Bay entirely.

During that day's run we repaired one puncture, broke and replaced the front engine chain—luckily we still had a spare—and despite these delays still managed to complete our crossing of the mighty and forbidding Nullarbor.

At Penong we were eagerly welcomed by a family and invited to stay for afternoon tea. After much posing for the photo-graphically minded members of the family, we headed off into the closer settled areas of Ceduna and Wirrula.

Now clear of the heavy sand country, we quickly built up

speed to 35 to 40 miles per hour. Around dusk we passed Yardea Sands homestead without so much as slackening speed. The occupants rushed out in time to see little more than our dust as we sped by. We were still averaging 200 miles a day. A waterhole shown on the map fifteen miles beyond Yardea homestead was dry, but we had to make camp there. Luckily we had sufficient water, just, to make a damper for supper.

Of course we were very pleased with our progress since leaving Perth, and kept up a high speed hour after hour, from daylight till dark. But soon we were in for a rude shock which nearly put an end to the whole adventure. In fact we seemed to enter upon a phase of bad luck, for a series of mishaps took place pretty well within a few hours of each other.

As usual, I was in the saddle from daylight till noon—'noon' being judged by the position of the sun, together with conditions suitable for preparing lunch.

As I sped along, a lonely tree stood fair in my path as I approached a fork in the road. I was still trying to decide which fork to take when I hit that tree a glancing blow with the sidecar wheel. I had half figured out that to go left would throw too much strain on the sidecar chassis—which was already cracked and only temporarily repaired—and was judging the wisdom of swerving to the right when ... Smack! The sidecar which took that lonely tree quite by surprise, which in turn took us by surprise. By some miracle the tyre and tube remained intact and, although the wheel was badly buckled, we could still carry on. Our speed had to be greatly reduced, but at least we were still mobile.

Not long later there was another setback to our steady progress. And we knew at once that this was more serious.

17

Serious Trouble

HAVING RACED across the Nullarbor Plain, we fancied we could already hear the plaudits of the crowd at our unprecedented success, when out of the blue there came a terrific knocking from the motor. This, coupled with the sidecar encounter with the tree only half an hour earlier, quickly erased our fanciful thoughts. There was no doubt about it. We were in real trouble this time. The buckled sidecar wheel was nothing compared to that ominous knock, knock, knock.

We quickly dismantled the engine and it didn't take long to determine the problem—a broken con rod. We looked at each other with such forlorn expressions that we both finished up bursting into laughter. In circumstances such as these some people seek to express their emotions with tears, but we found the opposite to be just as effective.

At least now we knew the worst. We were still 75 miles from Port Augusta, the nearest town and rail head to Adelaide, a further 200 miles away. We had no hope of getting a con rod between here and Adelaide. All the homesteads we had passed during the previous day or two were deserted—the occupants having packed up and left due to the prolonged drought. In fact we had seen no one for days, least of all travellers who may have been able to get a message through to the Harley agents in Adelaide.

Everything looked hopeless. We might be stuck out in the wilderness with our useless machine for weeks. Even if we could contact Adelaide, there was still the problem of how to get the spare parts over almost 300 miles of mostly isolated country.

'Where are we?' I asked Frank, who was reclining in the

sidebox, unable to take his fascinated gaze off that wickedly rotating buckled sidecar wheel.

Placing his finger on the map spread across his knees, he said, 'About here'. And 'here' was a small square indicated with the letters 'H.S.'

'H.S.' plus a square meant 'Homestead', and upon looking for the first time since that ominous knocking sound, there, full within our view through the scattered timber was a homestead. It stood there as if it had suddenly just been deposited for our special assistance. It is nice to think that God looks upon one favourably from time to time.

We lost no time in determining if this homestead, was deserted, like most of the others dotted back across the Nullarbor. But as we drew nearer we saw an aeroplane just sitting there, as if awaiting something to do. This sight pleased us immensely. Next, we noted telegraph lines stretching from the homestead into the far distance in the general direction of Port Augusta, and Adelaide. Now all we had to do was to present our case and plead assistance.

Walking up to the rear of the homestead we were met by the rouseabout, and that suited us fine. We always liked some form of buffer between ourselves and the owner, who may look down upon two such lowly, dishevelled, unwashed hobos as we.

'Wait here, I'll see the boss,' said the rouseabout. 'The morning tea bell'll go in a minute. Duck in and get a cuppa.'

However, before the tea bell rang he reappeared with the boss, who gave us the once over, and said he'd ring Adelaide. He then led us into his commodious homestead to the main dining room where stood the governess and the maid, to whom we were introduced.

Sitting on the very edge of those dining room chairs in our dusty leather riding breeches, we partook of refreshment delicately poured and handed to us by the young and beautiful governess. Meanwhile the boss said, 'Looks like you'll be here for a few days. I'll show you to your quarters, then we'll take the "pickup" over and tow your machine in.' He told us later that, unshaven and dirty as we had appeared, he had noticed our white teeth. And that is why we always ate with him in the dining room, waited upon most handsomely by the maid and the governess, the lady of the house being temporarily absent.

We retrieved our 'other clothes' from the sidebox—the outfit reclining quietly in the machinery shed—and lost no time in showering, shaving and donning standard apparel. This raised our egos somewhat and allowed us to sit more comfortably on those dining room chairs.

We had phoned Adelaide and received the promise that our spare parts would be put on that day's train for Port Augusta. It was left to us how to arrange delivery from there. But here again our good samaritan friend came to the rescue by borrowing a motor cycle from a neighbouring property.

Our quarters proved to be in a detached building known as the schoolhouse. Here we felt relaxed and pleased to escape the unaccustomed formalities observed in the main dining room with the beautifully arranged cutlery, doilies, and uniformed maid, and the small hand bell to which she responded.

Before retiring to our beds for the night and still being unfamiliar with the sanitary arrangements within the schoolhouse, we retired outdoors and proceeded to urinate and break wind in true masculine fashion. Our vigorous performance triggered off a fit of laughter at the end of this adventurous day.

The next morning as we appeared for breakfast the governess said, 'What was all that noise and hilarity outside my window last night?' This was a severe blow to our equanimity and we wished we were back in the spinifex on the treeless Nullarbor plain, sleeping like two dogs under the stars with our boots under our heads as pillows.

However, she had got the message across and we refrained from emulating drafthorses outside ladies' windows from that moment.

While we waited for the spares to arrive at Port Augusta we just spent much of the time sitting idly around the machinery shed and talking of this and that with our host.

During one of these conversations the boss said, 'That's a

nasty looking sidecar wheel, you've got there'. When we told him the story of how it became so nasty looking, he told us there was an old sidecar up in the shed that somebody had left there on their way across to Perth years ago.

We lost no time in inspecting the abandoned sidecar and to our good fortune found the wheel to be exactly the same size as our own. The axle bearing was slightly different, but with our usual resourcefulness we quickly overcame that problem by making a sleeve for it.

Once again the good Lord had smiled benignly upon us, and all we had to do now was obtain the new con rod and lose no time in getting that motor going again.

18

On the Road Again

DURING OUR enforced delay of three days we not only fitted the new con rod but overhauled the motor generally, saw to it that all the fencing-wire improvisations were in good shape, adjusted the various plates and shackles holding broken and cracked parts together, checked out the extra support to the cracked sidecar chassis which had been fitted in the smithy's shop at Moora-Bulla Aboriginal station more than 1,000 miles back along the track, and rejoiced in having our newly acquired sidecar wheel in situ after having bushed the axle bearing down in size to fit our original axle.

Roadworthy once again, and bound for Adelaide, we said our goodbyes, jumped on the kick-starter and were off.

Within two miles there came a terrific burst of noise from the engine. What now, we wondered. More trouble? No. Just that we had not connected one of the exhaust pipes securely enough to the cylinder head and it had come adrift. That was simply rectified in a few minutes, and off we went once more.

We stopped in Port Augusta only long enough to refuel and replenish the food supply, which left us with next to no money in the communal money belt. In fact we had been reduced to such a low ebb financially that when we were approaching Adelaide we could only afford either one gallon of petrol and one quart of oil, or two gallons of petrol, and one pint of oil. And having finally made our choice we had only tenpence-half-penny left. Of course we still had to pay for the spares we had received from the Harley agency in Adelaide.

However, not to worry. We expected to receive another small amount in the mail upon our arrival in Adelaide.

124

Meanwhile we had put away the miles since leaving our friends at the sheep station and as darkness fell found that we were only 90 miles from Adelaide so we decided to carry on. The evening meal was not necessary. We had eaten well over the past three days and we rode through the night on a well-formed road with our hand-held torch to light the way. Around midnight one tyre became flat and brought us to a halt, whether we liked it or not.

Some three or four miles out of Adelaide the next morning we were met by a motorcyclist escort to lead us into town. He proved to be a most nimble fellow, mounted solo on a speedy machine, and he tore off at such a speed that we had difficulty in keeping him in sight, especially when we were from time to time halted by policemen directing the traffic at intersections. They in their flat-topped caps appeared as funny to us as we must have done to them.

However, our wily escort evidently kept a keen eye on things through the back of his head, and saw to it that we both arrived at Lamroc's, the Adelaide Harley-Davidson agency together. Here we were met by the manager, who marvelled at the speed in which we had covered the distance without lights. He failed to see how we could have ridden so many miles throughout the night with only a small hand-held torch and upon such a hard ridden piece of machinery such as ours.

He was also fascinated by the tales we told of how we struggled from place to place on such a haphazard system of obtaining fuel and oil without prior organization.

We told him how at one place, somewhere near the Northern Territory and Western Australian border, we found an isolated windmill together with a can of windmill oil. As oil was one of the greatest costs, along with petrol, we filled our oil tank up with windmill oil—thick, black, windmill oil like treacle. Now and again we would pump some through with the oil hand pump just to make sure it was still flowing.

The manager kept on interrupting this and other stories with requests for more detail and it soon became obvious he wanted to write our story up and submit the most adventurous sections

to the American publication, *The Harley-Davidson Enthusiast.*
The magazine did pay our trip some attention.

We had received our slender sum of money at the post office,
Adelaide; enough, we hoped, to meet our immediate demands
and see us back to Sydney. The enthusiastic agency manager
was anxious to set us on the road as quickly as possible,
because, as he said, 'You've got the fastest time record in the
bag, you might as well make it as good as you can. That'll
make it that much harder to beat.'

We were reasonably content to rest on our achievement on
being the 'first'—a record which could not be taken ever—but
we also were anxious to be home. The most adventurous sections of the journey were behind us and what lay ahead of us
was just 'ordinary motoring'. Nevertheless we took the manager's advice and after being shown quickly around Adelaide we
made arrangements to check out the following morning.

Sunday morning we met the manager and his wife, who were
to escort us out of the city. He had prepared an itinerary of
day-to-day distances between Adelaide and Melbourne—mileages he thought should be suitable for each day's run, allowing
for the tired old bike doing its laborious best.

As we went along in our small procession the manager, who
was equipped with a small movie camera, took footage of our
historic departure. At the 25-mile mark, with much hand-
shaking and advice on the roads ahead, he took his leave.

We had been champing at the bit for those 25 miles, due to
our sluggish progress while the film-making was in progress,
so as soon as we were on our own once more we opened up
the throttle and doubled our speed.

Towards dusk we ate our evening meal, and since the road
was quite well defined although reasonably rough we decided
to keep going for another few miles before camping, to make
up for that slow exit out of Adelaide. Apparently the Harley
manager who set the pace thought our old bike could do no
better.

About 95 miles from Adelaide we made camp for the night
near the northern end of The Coorong. Early the next morning

we were off once more. Melbourne was about 400 miles ahead of us but we were already quite some miles ahead of our schedule. We rode all that day as usual, passed through Mount Gambier some four or five hours ahead of schedule, and as darkness began to fall we decided to ride on.

There was a half moon so we ate first, then prepared ourselves for a long night's riding. As the nights were still cold, both the rider and sidecar passenger wrapped a blanket around his upper body and buckled his riding coat over the top. With our little torch used more to indicate that we were a vehicle than as illumination, we rode all night on a good road and called a halt only when we were 90 miles from Melbourne on a beautiful sealed-surface highway.

At Geelong we stopped long enough to ask the Harley agent to see if the Melbourne people could send a guide out of the city to lead us in. Thus satisfactorily catered for in this regard, we were welcomed to the city of Melbourne.

We had covered 375 miles since the last camp, and clipped almost two days off the Adelaide manager's schedule. This gave us great satisfaction, and since the manager was such an enthusiastic motorist we proudly surprised him by sending a telegram immediately to say we had arrived. Knowing full well that we had no headlights he must have wondered what miracle had sped us on our way.

19

Journey's End

MELBOURNE IS ONLY 500-odd miles from Sydney. Although Frank and I had journeyed extensively around New South Wales, we had never before been this far south.

Now here we were, being escorted through the maze of streets and traffic, to the head office of the Harley-Davidson agents, Milledge Bros, where we were duly received and once again urged to keep up the good work. So after a cursory sight-seeing view of the city streets we were left to our own resources and, returning to our hotel room, lay down for a rest before lunch.

We awoke to find the room in darkness and to our astonishment found it was 9 p.m., so we undressed and climbed into bed. We didn't stir until the following morning—the day of our newly rescheduled departure for Sydney and home. The Harley dealers were certainly keen for us to set a speed record as well. Our plan was to arrive in Sydney on Saturday, late morning or early afternoon.

Leaving Melbourne, we found the road to be excellent for 70 or 80 miles. That night we camped on the roadside with a roaring fire. Up again and on the road early in the morning, we passed hundreds of swagmen who all appeared to be travelling in the same direction. We had never seen so many swaggies before and remarked that they must all be going to a swaggies' convention. I suppose now their numbers had more to do with the economic climate of September 1929.

That afternoon we came across two women battling with a flat tyre, which we changed for them. Little did they know that we were supposed to be record-breaking until one noticed 'Around Australia', barely discernible through the mud and dust, emblazoned on our sidecar. It was just another day to us, and we were in fact more than a month ahead of the fastest previous time. So why not finish as we had started, in a leisurely fashion?

When we crossed the border into New South Wales once again we almost considered ourselves in Sydney, although our starting point was still about 400 miles away. But what distance was that to us after covering about 9,300 miles since we left our home state fewer than three months ago?

Upon our arrival at Goulburn, 120 miles from Sydney, the Harley-Davidson agent was waiting for us. He took us to his office and soon we were talking to the Sydney Harley agents. Then we phoned family and friends and arranged to meet them at a well-known picnicking spot at the foot of Razorback. Here we proposed to make our last camp, and left Goulburn for the 80-mile run to the little running stream at the foot of the mountain which was to be our rendezvous.

We were looking forward to a happy gathering. At least two carloads of friends were on their way to meet us, but as we rode into this camp site we saw a couple already in occupation. They were a husband and wife whose motorcycle had broken down, and they were simply at a loss at what to do next. We discussed their situation with them and finally decided we would, first of all, eat. Then we would mount up and distribute their gear as best we could. I would sit behind Frank on the same saddle, the lady would sit in our sidebox while her husband rode their cycle behind in tow.

In the total darkness we set off. We still had our torch to flash on at the approach of an oncoming vehicle, but it was useless as far as illuminating the road surface was concerned. And thus we passed our friends in the dark. They ultimately found us camped in low scrub on the roadside, just fifteen miles out of Sydney. We had lodged the unfortunate motorcycling wayfarers at Camden, where they could at least obtain some accommodation for the night.

More and more friends converged on our camping spot and at sun-up the forbidding area began to look like a picnic gathering. But who on God's earth would pick on this spot for a picnic? Well, Frank and I would. We had camped at far far worse spots than this. In fact we were within three miles of my home, yet here I was in the early morning light shaving my face, combing my hair and changing my shirt, not more than a few yards from the main roadway. It was a desolate place in which to make oneself presentable for our triumphant home-coming at the Sydney GPO. There we knew would be Saturday morning crowds thirsting for any diversion that may eventuate. We didn't let them down as we drove our battered selves up in our battered outfit and made a stop in Martin Place, where the final stamping and signing of our card was to be completed. It was 21 September 1929.

The crowd was large and it soon became larger still. Once more came the usual questions. 'What are the roads like up north?' 'Are you getting anything out of this?' 'Have you had many punctures?' A police sergeant handling one of our boomerangs 'belonga Kimberleys' announced to everyone within earshot that he could 'throw one of these things' and poised the weapon with deadly intent, as if to threaten the facade of a huge building some distance away. Much to our gratification, however, he restrained himself and replaced the missile back where he had found it.

Upon the final stamping and signing of our card, which by now bore stamps and signatures from all the capital cities in the Commonwealth of Australia, our mission was ended. We could now go home and sleep in a proper bed and dispense with our plain flour, cream of tartar and soda, put our firearms away without fear of molestation by man or beast and lead an ordinary life once again.

Despite the hazards of the last eleven weeks—sleeping in the open under all sorts of conditions, drinking water in which lay dead cattle, and living from day to day always dependent on our skill in handling that heavy, unwieldly outfit in all manner of motoring hazards—despite all these hazards we had made it.

We had returned triumphant and were not only the first to circumnavigate Australia on a motorcycle and sidecar, but the fastest for any type of motorised land vehicle. We had also dispelled all doubts those cautious potential sponsors had about man not being able to live with man for long periods of isolation. We really felt as though we had achieved something. And that's a great feeling.

Over the following weeks we rode around the circuit at speedway races, lumbering around amidst squeaks and rattles which were nonetheless soft music to our well-adjusted ears. However, allow one small additional noise to appear amidst the rest and we would be alert like fox terrier dogs, ears cocked, tense, and ready to do battle against this intruder into our world of squeaks, snaps and rattles.

On one occasion we were invited to appear at a Rugby League football match. We rode up to the entrance gates, sought and gained admittance, but decided to leave our machine outside before checking the layout. Clad in our riding breeches, jackboots and riding coats we set out to find our sponsor. Suddenly there was loud clapping and a few cheers. We wandered over to the fence to see who had scored.

In fact it took some time to realise that it was Frank and I who were being acclaimed. We had apparently been observed by our sponser, who had got someone to make an announcement over the public address system—all beyond our hearing. How very nonchalant we must have appeared to the multitude as we casually leaned on that fence.

However the rush of children, and adults too, all armed with paper and pencil soon brought us back into the world of reality. Had we even had the slightest suspicion that the cheers and hand-clapping were in our honour we'd have probably turned and fled for the safety of our trusty machine. But we were really too vulnerable on foot. Our escape system was not speedy enough without the third member of our party—the Harley-Davidson.

Index